STRAIGHT FROM THE HEART

A Mother Battles Paranoid Schizophrenia, and a Girl Struggles to Grow Up

by

Carolyn H. Miller

authorHOUSE™

1663 LIBERTY DRIVE, SUITE 200
BLOOMINGTON, INDIANA 47403
(800) 839-8640
WWW.AUTHORHOUSE.COM

First published by AuthorHouse 4/11/2006

ISBN: 1-4208-4732-5 (sc)

Library of Congress Control Number: 2005904251

Printed in the United States of America
Bloomington, Indiana

This book is printed on acid-free paper.

CONTENTS

MEMORY OF SUMMER   1
THE RIDE   41
NEW BEGINNINGS   47
THE INCIDENT   77
FAREWELLS MUST COME   91
ONE DANCE   107
AFRAID TO LOVE   113
NOW AND FOREVER   145

MEMORY OF SUMMER

Sarah sat reminiscing of the summer she turned fifteen, the one that had helped shape her life. Lost in her memories of the past it seemed like only yesterday. The year was 1949, four years after the ending of World War II. Fifty years had passed since that memorable summer. Time may have blurred the sharpness of familiar faces, stolen the freshness of emotions she'd long since experienced, but not erased them.

School had just closed for the year and the heat was already upon them. Peter, Sarah's older brother by eleven years, was on summer break from seminary, and had invited her to spend her summer vacation with him and his family. The two country churches of which he was pastor shared him for bi-weekly Sunday services, and for Wednesday night prayer meetings. The extra salary helped with his school expenses while at seminary and during the winter months he drove back and forth on weekends.

Peter met Sarah in Grove Hill, a combination bus station-post office-grocery store, similar to those of other small towns located in the area. It was the closest bus station to Coffeeville, Alabama, where Peter's pastorates were, and where he and his family lived during the summer.

Exhausted and hungry after her all-day journey, she stepped from the bus and smiled at her brother. They hugged each other, and after collecting her luggage, Peter ushered her into the small eatery tucked into one corner of the station. They sat down at a glass-topped table and ordered sandwiches, with coffee for Peter and a cola for Sarah.

"How was your trip?" Peter asked.

"Fine, but I've never seen so many miles of farm land, pine trees, pastures, and just plain hills in my life," she sighed.

She was glad to see their food arrive, and took a big swallow of her cola and a bite of her sandwich. The food and drink were beginning to revive her, although she still felt half-dazed from the humming of the bus engine, and the constant vibration of tires as they clicked off the miles.

"You'll feel better after a good night's sleep," he assured her, patting her arm affectionately.

"How are Lois and Kelly? How far is it to where you live?"

Peter held up his hand. "Whoa, one at a time, please!" he said, laughing.

"They're doing just fine. They're looking forward to seeing you. And the ride home is only a few miles."

Sarah smiled gratefully, leaning her elbows on the table. Peter had finished eating, so she hastily swallowed her last bite of sandwich and gulped down the rest of her cola. She longed for a hot shower and a soft bed.

His expression changed from teasing to serious. "I have to warn you, it's no palace. We do have running cold water but no hot, as we don't have a water heater. We heat water, and cook on a kerosene stove. There's an outside toilet, but we do have an inside bathtub. Even though we're pretty far out in the sticks I think you'll get by. You may even enjoy it!"

He winked at her woebegone expression, and she smiled at him in return. They climbed into his aging sedan and soon arrived at the simple four-room structure. It consisted of two bedrooms, the front one being a combination living room and bedroom. The other bedroom was between it and the kitchen. Lois, Peter's wife, had remained home with Kelly, their four-year-old daughter. Sarah and Peter entered the house through the kitchen to keep from disturbing them.

"We use the chamber pot, or slop jar, at night. Finding your way to the outside toilet in the dark is a little too venturesome, even with a flashlight," he said.

Sarah looked at him and nodded in rueful agreement.

Her small bedroom adjoined Peter and Lois's. The chamber pot Peter had just described was tactfully placed next to her bed. Sarah caught a glimpse into the other room and saw Lois asleep in the double bed. Kelly slept on a daybed pushed against one wall.

"I'm beat," Sarah said with a yawn. "Good night."

The next morning when Sarah awoke, refreshed after her night's rest, the sun was already up. She splashed water on her face and rinsed her hands. As she hurriedly dressed she could smell the tantalizing smell of bacon and coffee. The aromas drew her to the kitchen where she was thrilled to find bacon, scrambled eggs, toast, and orange juice waiting for her.

"Hungry?" greeted Lois with a smile and set a place for her next to Kelly. Sarah enthusiastically nodded her head, then turned to her blonde-haired, blue-eyed niece sitting next to her.

"Kelly, I believe you've grown at least two inches in the months since I've seen you!" She gave the child a hug.

"Hi, Sarah," greeted the little girl with a wide grin.

Dressed in a blue-flowered playsuit Kelly seemed prepared for the day, and the temperature already promised both heat and humidity. The windows were held open with a "window stick" and Sarah could feel a little cool air coming through the screens. Pots of water that were conveniently obtained from the small sink were on the kerosene stove getting hot, and would be used for cooking, washing dishes, and, later, the laundry. Sarah felt its heat, and smelled the peculiar, but not objectionable odor of burning kerosene. After they finished eating, Peter pushed back from the table and gave Lois an affectionate kiss on the cheek.

"I'm going to pick up the mail," he told her. There was no local mail delivery, but it was sorted into the individual boxes at the nearby post office for pick up. It was within walking distance of the house.

After she and Lois had cleared the table, Lois set two aluminum dishpans on the table, which was the only available workspace.

"Want me to rinse and dry them for you?" offered Sarah.

Lois smiled at Sarah and replied," I never turn down an offer of help."

As Sarah began rinsing and drying the dishes Lois told her, "The dishes go in that cabinet against the wall over there," indicating a cabinet directly across from them.

"Pots and pans go on those two shelves under the stove. Peter built them for me. He's handy with a hammer and nails and am I glad!"

When they finished the dishes, Lois went to the pantry, and opened the door to remove the broom and dustpan.

I don't know what I'd do without my pantry. I keep my broom, dustpan, mop and mop bucket, iron and ironing board, and other odds and ends in it. It's a lifesaver."

"I can see why."

As she swept the floor Lois resumed their conversation. "Today is laundry day. Unfortunately, it has to be done by hand since I don't have a washing machine. I've found that pre-soaking the clothes in cold water makes the job easier. Tell you what, while I put them to soak why don't you let Kelly give you the grand tour?" she smiled at her own joke and Sarah smiled back.

"Okay. Come on Kelly, lead on," Sarah directed Kelly.

She had been sitting in her chair at the table, all the while silently taking in every word of their conversation. Kelly took Sarah's hand and they walked outside for a look at Sarah's new surroundings. As they turned the front corner of the house they heard chugging noises approaching from town.

The town consisted of a post office, service station, and a general store that sold everything from hardware and farm supplies to dry goods and grocery items. An old red tractor came into view driven by a boy around sixteen years old. He was dressed in a worn checked shirt, scuffed cowboy boots, faded brown pants, and a wide-brimmed straw hat. As he turned into the driveway of the house directly across the road from them, he threw up his hand in friendly greeting.

"That's Charlie Cotton. He has a sister nine years old. She plays with me sometimes. Her name is 'Sis,' " Kelly told Sarah.

Sarah's interest was piqued at the sight of one of her neighbors. She saw that she was going to be living in real country where most of its inhabitants farmed for a living, worked hard, and put in long hours. Sarah noticed his dark tan, but the hat pulled down over his eyes concealed most of his features. Still, she saw enough to be curious. She wondered which one of her brother's churches he attended, and the possibility of seeing him again both excited and frightened her.

Would a city girl fit in and be accepted by these people? She had no way of knowing.

She heard Lois calling for them.

"We're coming," Sarah called.

Holding Kelly's hand they rounded the back of the house to where the small back porch joined the bathroom.

"Do you need some help with the wash?" Sarah wished to be of help instead of a burden to them during her visit.

"Of course! As I said before, I never turn down help."

Lois began wringing out the linens and under things from their cold-water soak. Sarah hurried to help while Kelly remained outside to play. When the clothes were all wrung, soap powder and hot water from the stove were added, moderated with cold water for the right temperature.

"This is a back-breaking job isn't it?" signed Sarah.

"Yes, it is but it's not so bad when you're used to it."

Soon their efforts were rewarded by the sparkling white wash pinned to the metal clothesline. The sun would dry it in a matter of hours.

"We'll fold the clothes into that clothes basket when they are dry. Monday is washday and Tuesday I iron," explained Lois.

Sarah was beginning to feel a deep admiration for her sister-in-law's efficiency. Next they tackled a pile of dirty, colored garments and Lois finished outlining the rest of her weekly duties as Sarah helped with the rest of the laundry. Soon it was flapping on the line along with the other finished wash.

"Usually one big wash like this will take care of the week's laundry. In case of rain I have another clothesline inside this extra room, plus a wooden clothes rack for the smaller things." Lois pointed to the large room that was just off the bathroom—used for storage, drying laundry in wet weather, and a playroom for Kelly on rainy days.

"The cotton garments such as shirts, dresses, blouses, etc., I starch before hanging out to dry, as we just did today. Then I'll dampen them and roll them up in a pillowcase, to store in the refrigerator until the next day to keep them from drying out. Sometimes if I don't get them finished, I return them to the refrigerator until I can get back to them."

As they started into the kitchen suddenly Sarah's stomach growled loudly. Lois heard it and smiled.

"I'm beginning to get hungry, too. We'll fix a quick lunch. I'll make your favorite tuna salad sandwiches, and let you fry the squash. We can heat up some leftover green beans from yesterday, and there are tomatoes to slice. How does that sound?"

"Fantastic! I could eat anything right now. Why don't I peel these peaches and put sugar over them?"

"Oh, yes, please. That is Peter and Kelly's favorite dessert. I have half a cake that will go well with the peaches."

" I can't wait to taste them. They look just soft enough to be good."

Soon the table was set and the meal ready to eat. Moments later, Peter walked in. He picked up Kelly, who had come in with him, and tickled her ribs before putting her into her chair. She giggled with pleasure at his attention.

"Any mail for me?" asked Lois. Peter glanced through the mail he had deposited on the end of the table. "Yes, you've a letter from your mother."

"Oh, good. I've been worried because I hadn't heard from her for so long," she exclaimed eagerly, reaching for her letter. They sat down and made short work of the delicious meal. As they pushed back their chairs from the table Sarah said firmly," Lois, you sit down in the shade somewhere and read your letter, and Kelly and I'll do the dishes."

Lois thankfully obeyed and was soon seated under the large pecan trees at the far side of the house. The trees provided an abundance of cool protection from the sun. Peter went into the front room, where there was a small desk. He returned to the kitchen with a sermon he had begun working on.

"Sarah, how about looking at this when you two finish the dishes. I haven't finished it yet, but I think it's a good beginning." Peter handed it to her before she got her hands wet with dishwater.

"I'd be glad to, Peter." She laid it carefully on an empty, dry corner of the table. He walked on out to the front porch to sit in his favorite rocking chair to peruse the weekly issue of the local newspaper, and to look through the rest of the day's mail.

Kelly was in a silly mood, and soon Sarah was infected with it also. They took their time cleaning up, Sarah singing some of the folk songs she'd learned in fifth grade while Kelly attempted to follow along, often misunderstanding the words and fracturing them until they were overcome with laughter.

"You're funny, Sarah," gasped Kelly as she tried to stop laughing.

"So are you, kiddo," returned Sarah, wiping her eyes with the back of her hand. They soon had the kitchen in good order and went out to join Lois under the pecan trees.

"Oh, I forgot Peter's sermon."

"I'll get it for you, Sarah," offered Kelly, running back into the house. She returned with it in her hand, a little damp, but whole.

"Thanks, Kelly!"

Sarah settled down to read Peter's sermon, and Kelly sat on the ground to play in the sandy soil with empty pecan hulls and twigs from the trees overhead to draw patterns in the dirt. Lois had laid her head against the back of her chair and was dozing with her mother's opened letter in her lamp. There was a peaceful silence as all enjoyed their individual pursuits.

Sarah finished reading Peter's sermon. His text was the story of the prodigal son, and she could feel the love and sincerity with which he'd written his half-finished sermon. She decided to tell him how good it was. She went into the house to the front room. A small desk and bookcase tucked against the wall served as Peter's study.

"Peter, your sermon is off to a wonderful start. I never realized what a gift you have for explaining the Scriptures. But I've never heard you preach, have I?" Peter looked up at his sister with a warm smile.

"No, I don't believe you have, at that. That's soon going to change, isn't it?" he teased.

"That has always been one of my favorite stories in the Bible. I'm glad it will be in the first revival sermon I'll hear you preach."

"Well, thanks, Sis. You know the revivals aren't too far away and, of course, Bible school will begin in a couple of weeks. Think you'll want to help?"

"Oh, sure! I've always enjoyed attending Bible school."

Peter gave her a quick hug. They turned as Lois and Kelly entered the room.

"I wondered where you two had gotten to," Lois said. She laid her mother's letter on the corner of Peter's desk, and placed her hand on his shoulder.

"I just came to congratulate Peter on the sermon he's preparing for the revival," explained Sarah. "It's very good."

"Well, on behalf of my wonderful husband, I thank you," said Lois. She smiled at Peter and leaned over to drop a kiss on his hair.

Kelly looked from one to the other, sensing they were discussing something important but not understanding it.

She entreated Sarah, "Will you make a paper doll and clothes for me, Sarah, please? Yours are better than the bought ones."

"Well, thanks, kiddo. Sure. We'll get your paper, pencils, crayons, and scissors and get started before it's time to fix supper."

"We'll need some glue, too, won't we? "

"Yep, and some cardboard, too, so she'll stand up," reminded Sarah. Soon they were engrossed at the favorite work place, the kitchen table. Sarah made the paper doll, cutting it out for Kelly, whose small fingers weren't quite skillful enough for such a tedious undertaking.

While they were working, Lois came into the kitchen and smiled at them. "I once liked to play with paper dolls. Money was tight in our family so I learned to make my own. Most of the bought ones were pictured after my favorite female movie stars."

"Oh, I remember those! I learned to make my own, also, as you did. Betty Grable, Lana Turner, Ava Gardner, and Esther Williams paper dolls," exclaimed Sarah.

"What are we having for supper?" asked Kelly as she watched Sarah carefully tracing around the doll to make her a dress. Tabs at the shoulder and waist would hold the doll's clothes onto her form.

"I thought we'd just have soup and sandwiches," answered Lois, who'd picked up the scissors and was cutting out one of the dresses Sarah had drawn and colored.

"Oh, goodie! Can we have chicken noodle with peanut butter and jelly?" begged Kelly.

"Well, since that is your all-time favorite why not?" Lois ruffled Kelly's hair.

With Lois's help they completed making the doll's clothes and Kelly began trying them on her. Lois and Sarah prepared the simple supper, and soon they were seated at the table. Before they began eating, Peter said grace.

"Which church will we be going to Sunday?" asked Sarah around her bite of peanut butter and jelly sandwich.

"We'll be going to Ulcanush, and next week West Bend," replied Peter.

Sarah offered, "I'll clean up these few dishes while you and Kelly have a story time, and get ready for bed. It'll only take me a minute."

"Okay, thank you. I think I'll get ready first, and then get Miss Kelly ready so she won't have as long to get dirty. She can play a few minutes while I get my bath," laughed Lois, holding her daughter's hand as they headed into the front room of the house. "Don't forget our devotion time," she reminded Sarah over her shoulder.

When Sarah had finished, the kitchen was spick and span and she went into her room to prepare for bed. As she pulled her shirt over her head, she heard someone enter the room and shut the door. Hurriedly, Sarah wiggled into her gown and held her housecoat in front of her.

"It's just me, Sarah," Lois reassured her. "I just wanted a few minutes alone with you."

"Oh, sure," replied Sarah in relief. "What is it?"

"When we washed the clothes today I didn't see a bra in with your things. Do you not wear one?"

Sarah flushed and began to pull the housecoat on over her gown.

"No. I suppose Mother hasn't realized that I'm not a baby, anymore. I guess I haven't found the right time or known what to say."

"Well, you really need to begin wearing one. We'll see about getting you a couple before Sunday. I also want to get some material for a new dress or two. With the revivals not too far away you need another couple of Sunday dresses."

Sarah flew over to Lois and hugged her in relief and gratitude. "Oh, Lois, thank you so much. I've felt so self-conscious, especially in shorts and a tee shirt." Lois returned her hug.

Sarah took a sponge bath of her own, brushed her teeth, and returned to the front room with the others for their nightly devotional time. After the Bible reading, each one was given a chance to pray aloud. It was a special time for Sarah, listening to Peter and Lois expressing their thoughts to God and trying to say what was in her own heart to her Heavenly Father.

Finally it was Sunday, and Peter drove them along the winding dirt road to Ulcanush Baptist church. Sarah felt more confident in the dress Lois had made, but she still felt a few butterflies, not really knowing what to expect. She knew this would be her first hurdle in getting to know the people with whom she would spend the next few weeks. Arriving at the church they climbed out of the car. She remembered the houses they had passed on their way, mostly unpainted, simple farm dwellings with the same type of bathroom that she was adjusting to. The only difference was that her brother's house was painted white. *Maybe there would be little to fear from people who lived in such humble dwellings.*

The church was a white frame structure with wooden steps leading up to the porch. There was a window on either side of the front door, and as Sarah entered behind Peter and his family, she was filled with trepidation. She followed Lois and Kelly and sat down on the plain, wooden pew beside two of her brother's parishioners. A pulpit stood on a raised platform in the front with a row of pews to one side for the choir, and the piano on the other.

As Lois introduced her to the women, Sarah noticed, to her surprise, that they treated them with a humble respect, bobbing their heads in greeting, and eyeing them surreptitiously.

Why they're just as shy as I am!

As others began to file into the church she noted that most of the women were dressed in simple cotton dresses, probably homemade. The men were dressed in dark or khaki pants with cotton sport shirts, their hair slicked back with hair tonic. Sarah guessed that some of the men's shirts were homemade also, possibly from chicken food sacks. She had seen the colorful sacks of chicken and hog feed at the general store, and admired the thriftiness and skill of the women who sewed their families' clothes.

As Peter stood and announced the hymn, her attention was directed back to the service.

Hearing the piano introduction she noted that the young pianist played the instrument with surprising skill. Hastily she fumbled through her hymnal for the correct page, then stood to sing with the congregation. Their voices rang with enthusiasm and a natural ear for music. Sarah joined her voice with theirs, and the reverent joyfulness with which they sang touched her. She felt a humble sense of God's presence in the simple setting, and it brought a mist to her eyes.

After the song ended, Peter stood once more, not at the pulpit, but at the front as if he wished to be on a level with the people. He asked for prayer requests, and several of the sick in the community were mentioned along with a family who had recently lost a loved one.

As the congregation silently prayed for those named, Sarah found herself praying along with them. Peter then gave a short message on prayer and how important it was in the lives of each of them, using the example of prayer in the life of Jesus as recorded in the Scriptures.

Before the service was dismissed, Peter reminded the congregation of the upcoming revival, and of Bible school which would begin in a couple of weeks. After a closing hymn, one of the men led in a simple but heartfelt prayer to close the services. Sarah's eyes were damp again, and as they filed out of the church she noticed that a few of the women's eyes were misted, as well, and felt a common bond with them. She was uplifted by the experience, and smiled as she greeted them..

Once outside, Lois introduced her to several of the women. They were grouped in front of the church for a time of fellowship, talking and laughing with each other, and enjoying being together. Kelly and other small children were running in a gleeful game of tag. Soon the group began to scatter and head for home. Most of the vehicles were trucks. If the family couldn't all fit into the front, the rest rode in the back.

Riding home with Peter, Lois, and Kelly, Sarah was silently contemplating the service and reveling in her newfound peace. "That's a nice church. The people seemed to enjoy the service and were friendly," Sarah commented.

"You sound as though you are surprised at our backwoods congregation," teased Peter, and smiled at her in his rearview mirror.

"Well, I guess you could say I was surprised," she agreed. "I really didn't know what to expect, but it was a good service and I enjoyed it."

"I'm glad. It will make things easier for you," replied Peter, satisfied.

"Let's go to town in the morning and get a home permanent," Lois decided, her thoughts evidently wandering to a different subject.

"Your hair has a nice texture but I think a loose curl would help it in this hot, humid weather."

"You can do home permanents, too?" asked Sarah, with amazement. "I don't believe there's anything you can't do."

"Oh, yes, there are a lot of things I can't do. But, like my mother always told me 'can't never could.' I try to do the things I can, and not worry about the things I can't," answered Lois, turning around to smile at Sarah over the back of her seat.

"If there's something I want or need to do, I always try my best to do it and, so far, her advice has worked pretty well."

Sarah was beginning to know her sister-in-law better, and saw Lois as a very down-to-earth, practical person who took Peter's ministry seriously, as well as her own role as a minister's wife. She had no idea that more serious days loomed ahead.

Lois took Sarah shopping for material and a bra the next morning. When they entered the general store, Sarah could not believe the variety of items that were available. "They've got everything from furniture to fresh meats and vegetables," she exclaimed.

"Yes, and it's nice to have everything in one place and not have to go to a dozen different stores," agreed Lois, smiling at Sarah's wide-eyed stares at each item she saw. Metal wash tubs with water and milk pails, hammers, and hatchets hung overhead. Not a bit of space was wasted, for what was not displayed on the floor of the building hung overhead. Sarah had shopped in the Department Stores at home that carried clothing, linens, curtains, cookware, shoes, and cosmetics. Each floor was stocked with related items. But this store had everything on one floor, with separate areas for the different wares.

They finally found the materials and sewing notions. Bolts of material were standing on end on tables and the price per yard marked each bolt. A pink eyelet caught Lois's eye and she fingered the cloth and unrolled a little to see more of the material before showing it to Sarah, who was turning through the pattern books.

"How do you like this pink eyelet, Sarah?" Lois asked, holding the unrolled material out for Sarah to see.

"Oh, I love it! Pink is one of my favorite colors. Do you like this pattern?" Sarah pointed to the pattern she'd selected. It was a sleeveless dress style with a yoke that buttoned down to a wide-banded waist, with a turn-back collar and softly gathered yoke and skirt.

"Oh, yes, that is nice, and it will be flattering since you're so slim."

Next they selected thread, buttons, and a zipper to match the material. Their next stop was the underwear displays where Lois showed Sarah a bra in a size that she thought would fit— which was the smallest size in ladies' bras. "I like these bras because they last well and are comfortable," Lois recommended.

"They look great to me," beamed Sarah. Lois selected two, along with the required yardage for the dress pattern, thread, buttons, and zipper for the back of the dress. Sarah was very excited. They strolled over to the hair items—combs, brushes, shampoos, conditioners, everything for the hair including home permanents.

"This is a good brand and it has everything in the box you need: waving lotion, neutralizer, end papers, and plastic curlers for rolling. I've used them on my own hair and usually get good results."

"Oh, goodie! Something for my thick, straight hair."

Sarah was enjoying the shopping trip to the fullest. They carried their selections over to the main counter and paid for everything, rather than having to purchase each item in a different department as she was used to at home. They saw Peter over in the grocery section. He had made several purchases as well. He joined them, and they were ready to go.

The next few days were spent sewing Sarah's dress and doing her hair. The waving lotion burned her eyes and skin in spite of the towel held to her face, but it was worth it when she saw the final results. The soft waves looked like natural curls, and flattered her fair complexion and brown eyes.

"Oh, I love it, Lois!" exclaimed Sarah as she examined the style in the mirror that hung over her chest of drawers. "It was worth all the discomfort." She turned to look at the back in the hand mirror she held.

"Oh, what price beauty," laughed Lois, a satisfied expression on her face as she viewed her efforts.

Lois cut another dress for Sarah while the latter washed up the dishes and swept and mopped the kitchen. The portable sewing machine hummed all afternoon. Sarah took Kelly outside to play. Sis Cotton came over when she saw the girls, and soon she and Kelly were playing with some large, black, speckled grasshoppers. They brought one to Sarah, who had never seen this particular kind. She was familiar with the small green grasshoppers, and they posed no threat to her. But these were huge, evil-looking creatures. Sis and Kelly laughingly chased Sarah with the horrid creature. Sarah squealed and ran from them, to their delight. Then Charlie and Frank came over leading a short, wide-backed horse.

"Want to ride?" Charlie asked Sarah when they neared the girls. Sarah looked with dismay at the unfamiliar horse, and down at her dress.

"I've never ridden horseback before," she replied, hoping to excuse herself. "I'm not dressed to ride, anyway," she continued, eyeing the horse with trepidation.

"Oh, she's easy to ride. I'll hold the halter for you," Charlie promised.

Sarah saw that the boys would take no excuse, so she clambered awkwardly onto the bare back of the horse, trying to modestly pull her dress down around her legs. She felt embarrassed because her slip kept showing in spite of her efforts to tug it and her dress down to cover her knees. The boys only grinned and began leading the horse slowly, and watching in amusement as Sarah braced her hands on each side and rocked with the horse's gait. The horse's back was too wide for Sarah's legs to hang down over its side, so she had to spread her knees to fit them around the horse's back, which only caused her dress and slip to ride up more. Her face burned with humiliation and she felt and looked uncomfortable. After a few more yards, the boys took pity on her and she gratefully climbed down as they held the horse's halter.

"I can ride Queenie bareback," bragged Sis, looking condescendingly at Sarah's awkward attempts to get off the horse without exposing too much of her legs.

"Th-Thanks for the ride," Sarah said politely, but secretly glad it was over.

"You're welcome," they grinned, pleased at their success in exposing her as a city girl come to the country. Sarah thought their smug expressions were a little too self-satisfied. She wished she had a way to retaliate but at the moment she could think of none. She was at a disadvantage and they knew it. Charlie and Frank waved goodbye as they led the horse back across the road.

Peter decided to have a few socials to help Sarah meet some of the young people of the community. The first one was an ice cream social, which was held at the summer parsonage. Lois made her famous pound cake and Peter made a churn of banana ice cream to go along with it. Several of those invited came, and after they had enjoyed the delicious refreshments, they played a game Peter had looked up in his thick game book.

"You boys want to help me bring some chairs outside under the light in the front yard?" Peter asked the boys, who were awkwardly standing together in the front room. He noticed them stealing glances at Sarah when they thought she wasn't looking.

"Sure," they answered, relieved to have something to do with their hands. Each of them carried a chair outside to the front yard. Peter asked them to arrange them in a circle at the edge of the yard. This gave sufficient light for them to engage in quiet games.

"The first game we'll play is called Scissors," announced Peter, holding up a pair of Lois's dressmaking shears. "Has anyone ever played this game before?" Each person shook his head so he began to explain the rules for the game. Several of the girls were seated with the boys in the circle and all listened eagerly to his explanation.

"I'm going to pass these scissors to my wife, and she will hand them to the person next to her, and so on around the circle. You can either say, I pass these scissors to you crossed, or I pass them to you uncrossed. Watch and listen carefully to see if you can figure out what determines why you say either crossed or uncrossed as you hand them to each other."

He looked at the scissors for just a moment as if to determine which was correct. Then he handed them to Lois, who in turn did the same before handing them to the person sitting next to her. Each of the guests watched closely as the game continued in order to attempt to discover the secret of the game. Sarah and the other young people kept the scissors going around the circle, their attention fixed on the instrument they were handling, but no one felt that they had guessed the secret.

After many rounds of the scissors around the circle and still no correct guesses, Peter asked them, "Do you give up?" Each person in the group either nodded his head or said a spoken "yes."

"If your legs are crossed, you pass the scissors as crossed, but if your legs are uncrossed you pass the scissors as uncrossed," Peter explained to them.

They were all disgusted at the simple solution that had stumped them for so long. Some of them groaned out loud in their disbelief that such a small detail had escaped them. Then they laughed, vowing that they were going to pull the same stunt on someone else. By this time it was growing late. Kelly had fallen asleep in Lois's lap, so one by one they began to stand.

"Guess we'd better call it a night," one of the boys said to Peter, and they began gathering up the chairs to carry them back into the house. Peter took Kelly from Lois and carried her inside while Sarah helped Lois gather up the remains of their refreshments.

"We had a good time, Preacher," one of the girls said as they turned to him for their goodbyes.

"Sure did," other voices echoed, their smiling faces reflecting their enjoyment of the evening.

"Glad you did," Peter replied, returning their smiles. As they turned to leave, Peter promised them, "We'll plan another social before too long."

"Okays" and "goods" were heard as the young people turned to wave their thanks. Peter looked at Sarah as he closed the door.

"Did you enjoy it, Sarah?"

"Oh, it was great! I think everyone had fun," she answered, trying to hide a yawn behind her hand.

"I believe it is bed time for all of us," agreed Peter, repeating her yawn openly. "Have you ever heard that a yawn is contagious?" he asked her as he switched off the front porch light.

"No, but I know that every time I see someone else yawn, I end up yawning, too, so it must be true. Good night, Peter, Lois," Sarah called over her shoulder to them as she started into her room. "I really had a nice time tonight. Thanks for having the social for me." She softly closed the door to keep from waking Kelly.

Since most of the young people from Ulcanush and the surrounding area had attended the ice cream social, West Bend Church's young people planned a social at their church for Sarah the following week. Peter was asked to help with the festivities, and it was decided to hold it on Friday night. Sarah was excited but a little apprehensive, too. Of course, Peter and Lois attended because there were very few functions that took place without inviting the preacher and his wife. The weather was cooperative—no thunderstorms threatened—and the fair skies of the day continued into the evening.

"Lois, what should I wear?" Sarah valued her opinion, knowing she was familiar with the church, its community, and its inhabitants.

"Why don't you wear that white batiste blouse and flowered chintz skirt you brought with you? It's not too casual nor too dressy, and you won't be too hot in that." The skirt was a broomstick skirt in the current fashion, gathered onto a waistband and a sash that tied in the back. Sarah had just starched and ironed it that week so it was clean.

"That's perfect! I can wear my brown sandals, too. They're a year old but still look okay as long as I keep them polished," agreed Sarah. Now that the question of her attire was settled Sarah felt less anxious, and washed and set her hair early in the day so it would be dry.

The crowd, which included many adults and children, gathered in the church. After refreshments were served, a game of "Cross Questions and Crooked Answers" was begun, led by Peter. This was a hilarious game with amusing questions that demanded ridiculous answers. No one came up with the correct answer. The answers in

Peter's game book weren't meant to be logical, but were designed to be funny and entertaining. The answers that the contestants gave were often just as funny as the "crooked answers" from the game book. Sarah relaxed, forgetting about herself, and wholly enjoying the game along with the others in attendance. After that game had played out, many of the adults with young children left to put them to bed, leaving most of the young folks to continue playing. Someone suggested a game of "Spin The Bottle," so Peter found an empty soft drink bottle to use for the game. By this time the group had retired to the inside in an attempt to escape the mosquitoes that came out in abundance at dusk and lingered long after nightfall. There were no screens over the windows so some of them managed to find their way indoors, but everyone was used to them, so they either swatted at them with their hands or simply ignored them. There were large bugs with hard-shell backs that entered the building, also, and Sarah kept one eye on them as they flew around the room, and one eye on the activities inside. She wasn't any fonder of them than she was of the large black grasshoppers!

The boys arranged chairs in a circle so the bottle could spin easily on the wooden floor. The object of the game was for the bottle to be given a spin by whoever was "it," so that its head would point toward someone when it had stopped revolving. This lucky person had to pay a penalty, and the spinner could name whatever penalty he or she desired. At first the penalties were silly things such as "crow like a rooster," "quack like a duck," and other animal imitations. Gradually, however, they began to be bolder, and the penalty for the person to whom the bottle pointed was asked to walk out to the graveyard with a person named from the opposite sex. Or it was to walk around the graveyard with the person's arm around their waist, as in the case of a girl paying the penalty.

Kelly had already stretched out on one of the pews and surrendered to sleep. Lois sat beside her to make sure she didn't roll off onto the floor.

Sarah made several trips back and forth to the graveyard and around the cemetery with various members of the male gender. It seemed like harmless fun to her, and felt perfectly natural for a boy to put his arm around her waist as they walked around the cemetery directly behind the church. There were lights at each corner of the church so the young people could see where they walked, preventing them from stumbling over a gravestone or marker and possibly hurting themselves. It didn't occur to her that anyone would make something objectionable of it until later...

After the social had ended she, Peter, Lois and a sleepy Kelly headed for home. Lois pointed out to Sarah in a critical tone that it didn't look right for her, as the preacher's sister, to be walking with a boy's arm around her waist in the cemetery after dark, especially as some of the young men were older.

"You're the preacher's sister and are supposed to set a good example to others. If they see you doing something questionable they'll think, 'well, if the preacher's sister can do it, then it's all right for me to do it.' " Lois' remarks were critical.

Sarah felt surprise, disappointment, and a little anger toward Lois for the first time in their relationship. Lois had taken what seemed a harmless, all-in-fun activity and made something forbidden and questionable of it. What made her feel worse was the fact that Peter had not called a halt to the game as it got a little "out of hand," as Lois put it, but remained silent, even now. As Lois continued with her critical comments of the game, the ones who participated in it, and the bolder activities that were engaged in as it had ended, Sarah's mixed feelings of being misunderstood and unfairly discriminated against left her shocked and speechless. Even if she could have put her feelings into words, she wouldn't have known how to express the depth of her emotions. Lois was demonstrating a different side of her personality and character to Sarah, and she had no defense against it.

Undeniably, she was the preacher's sister, and young as she was, she had to be different from the others. She was expected to set an example to those who would be watching her, looking to her for direction in how to behave in a Christian manner. She understood that Peter was a man of God, called to preach the Gospel and try to give light to others, and didn't want to behave improperly. Lois went on to impress upon Sarah the importance of correct behavior for a preacher's sister. Sarah's feelings were so overwhelming she felt powerless and knew of no way to explain or defend her actions. She simply listened and said nothing. She realized that Lois was speaking her version of the truth and she began to understand that her behavior had to be above reproach, for Peter's sake.

The next afternoon was still and sultry, and Sarah, Lois, Peter, and Kelly took refuge under the shade from the pecan trees. Chairs were carried outside, and Lois had made another fresh pound cake and some refreshing lemonade. As they relaxed in the shade and sipped the cool lemonade, Sarah saw Charlie Cotton approaching from across the road. Her heart fluttered as she took in his lean legs, supple waist, and the casual swing of his walk as he neared them. Peter made room for Charlie to sit in Kelly's chair, while she happily sat on the ground and played in the dirt.

Charlie sat down with unconscious ease and stretched out his long legs. He wore old brown pants and pointed cowboy boots. He pushed his straw hat back on his head and the sun, low on the horizon, shone straight into his face. Peter served him cake and lemonade, and he sipped the cool liquid gratefully. The sun's rays on his face gave his eyes a warm amber glow as he sat, relaxed, with an indolent grace that Sarah found extremely attractive.

Looking at his tawny eyes and lazy smile as he slouched in his chair with legs outstretched, Sarah suddenly felt a sharp spasm in her stomach, a new feeling she'd never experienced before. Instinctively, even in her youth, she recognized it as a response to the person sitting across from her, his dark hair and sinfully long eyelashes brought into sharp focus by the sun's rays. She felt an instant attraction to him, a pull that fascinated her, although she didn't identify it as anything sexual. Suddenly, he was incredibly appealing. He seemed older than before.

She'd always thought he looked nice enough. He was interesting and held her attention, but this was a much stronger feeling, that held her almost spellbound and confused her. She tried to hide her feelings from him, afraid and uncertain of her emotions and not sure how he felt toward her. He soon finished his glass of lemonade and stood, tall, and lanky against the blue sky. Until now he had been the interesting neighbor boy who she secretly watched when he'd pass on the tractor, a boy with whom she'd had little contact, until he'd teased her and made fun of her. But now…

"Could Sarah go with me to the picture show tonight? It's a new Roy Rodgers picture with Dale Evans and Gabby Hayes. It starts at seven o'clock," he asked, turning to look at Peter and then Lois.

Sarah was flabbergasted. She knew, of course, that there was a small, unpretentious movie theatre on Main Street in town, but she hadn't really noticed it that much. Peter glanced uncertainly at Lois, plainly surprised and unprepared to make such a decision. Clearing his throat Peter replied doubtfully, "I suppose she could, if she comes straight home afterwards. What time will you pick her up?"

"About a quarter 'til seven. We can walk to the movie. It's only three or four blocks away," Charlie assured them.

Thus Sarah's first date was arranged.

Charlie was prompt, arriving at quarter 'til seven o'clock on the dot. Sarah was ready in her white sleeveless blouse and red plaid skirt she'd ironed just that day, and her brown sandals.

It was a warm evening so she knew she'd be comfortable without any kind of wrap. Lois, Peter, and Kelly were in the living room when Charlie arrived and knocked at the door, even though the outside door was open with just the screen door closed. Peter went to the door.

"Hello, Charlie. How's it going? Won't you come in?"

"Hello, Preacher. I'm fine, thank you," Charlie replied entering the room as Peter held the door open for him. Kelly looked at Charlie with open interest.

"Do you and Sarah have a date?" She asked without compunction and the unabashed curiosity that all young children have.

"Uh, yes. I guess you could say that," Charlie replied, smiling at the little girl, but obviously a little taken back by her candor.

Just then Sarah came into the room and walked over to greet Charlie, who still stood just inside the entrance. "Ready?" he asked awkwardly.

"Yes, I guess so," she replied, feeling a little more at ease. She wanted to make him more comfortable, too, so she smiled at him and then turned to Peter and Lois.

"We'll probably be home before ten o'clock, don't you think so?" she asked, pausing to look inquiringly at Charlie.

"Yeah, sure. The movie probably won't last much over an hour and a half."

"Well, we'll see you all later," Sarah spoke, looking at Peter and then Lois. "Good night, Kelly," she smiled at the child, knowing she'd be asleep when she returned.

"Good night, Sarah," replied Kelly, who then added unselfconsciously, "Good night, Charlie."

"Good night, Kelly," Charlie answered, including all of them in his farewell glance. He opened the door then, and he and Sarah stepped off the porch without further words.

The sky still held that afterglow between daylight and darkness. The red sunset lingered on the horizon. Sarah looked at the beauty of the violet and faintly purple streaks which blended into the red-gold of the disappearing globe of the sun as it slowly slipped out of sight, and spoke, breaking the silence between them.

"What a lovely sunset."

"Yes, it is," agreed Charlie, following her gaze to the splendor before them as they wound their way to the theatre. His voice reflected his appreciation for the beauty of nature that comes only from working closely to the earth, and from one who had been exposed to the elements.

They came to the cemetery, which they had to pass on their way. "You're not afraid of ghosts, are you?" he teased her.

"No, not really. I know the people in there can't hurt us. It's only the people who are alive that we need to fear," she replied, with a touch of humor in her voice. "Although I do feel "spooky" sometimes when I hear ghost stories," she admitted, glancing at him in the glow of the streetlights. They were in sight of the theatre now, and she saw a few people standing in line at the entrance waiting to purchase their tickets.

He laughed at her admission, and they walked a few more steps, then paused to look both ways before crossing over to the theatre entrance. He pulled out his billfold and paid for two tickets from the lady in the ticket booth. Sarah didn't know her and looked questioningly at Charlie as they entered the theatre.

"That's Miss Johnson, Miss Phoebe Johnson," he told her in a low tone of voice as they entered the darkened theatre. Sarah had noticed the lady's glance of sharp interest as she looked at Charlie and then back to her when he bought their tickets. "She's a teacher at the high school," he continued, his voice still lowered to keep from disturbing the other theatre occupants.

Sarah let Charlie go first to select their seats on the wooden benches of the movie theatre. *At least there are backs to the benches.* Charlie paused politely to allow her to go first. She passed between the rows of benches and sat down close to the end of their bench. Another older couple joined them as they seated themselves. Sarah looked at the screen and noted that the preview of coming attractions was being shown. Most of them were detective shows or westerns, and after the previews were over, the movie came on.

Charlie had discreetly laid his arm along the back of the bench behind Sarah when they sat down, and as the movie played, his hand closed around the top of her bare shoulder. The picture starred Roy Rodgers and "Gabby" Hayes so there were plenty of humorous moments when Gabby shot humorous colloquialisms and excited questions in rapid fire. Roy Rodgers answered his queries calmly and with his own special style. He was the straight man who brought out the humor in each scene. In the end Gabby would always be the fall guy, either with "egg on his face," or being surprised at the outcome of the situation in question.

Charlie laughed heartily at the humorous scenes, using them as an excuse to edge closer to Sarah. Soon she began to feel his fingers lightly caressing her shoulder and arm, and she found it very enjoyable. She let it continue for a few more moments until the mental picture of Lois's face and the memory of her stern warnings that she was the preacher's sister, and as such must walk circumspectly before others for Peter's sake flashed through her mind. As much as she hated to, she knew she had to ask Charlie to remove his arm.

At first, she'd yielded to the temptation to flirt just a tiny little bit, turning to look at Charlie when he'd make a comment on the action or conversation in the movie, letting her eyes linger on his mouth for a few seconds to see what would happen. But her conscience refused to let her dally and to enjoy his attentions, and reluctantly she whispered, "Could you please move your arm?" Looking at her in surprise and chagrin he complied.

She was miserable through the rest of the movie. She hated that she had felt forced to go against her inclination to enjoy the feeling of his fingers caressing her shoulder, enjoying it but feeling guilty for doing so. His attentions felt so good, and she wanted so much to let it continue but she didn't dare do so. The plot and action of the movie were ruined for her, and she sat like a statue until it ended, glad she could escape at last the censoring eyes that she felt were on her. They moved out into the fresh evening air. It had been rather stifling inside the theatre, and she'd wiped away the sweat that had beaded upon her upper lip with her handkerchief more than once.

"Whew, it was hot in there, wasn't it?" she remarked after they were outside, not thinking about the way it probably sounded.

"It was plenty warm," agreed Charlie without looking at her.

It was a relief to Sarah to be walking off some of her tension, and she commented politely, "It was a good movie. I enjoyed it very much." She hoped that Charlie believed her.

"Yeah."

They walked more slowly as they got away from the edge of town toward her house. Sarah looked up at the stars that seemed so close. The clean country air magnified their brilliance.

"The stars look so much bigger and brighter here than at home."

In the town where she lived the soot and smoke from the many textile mills in the area was so thick at night you could actually smell it, and the sky always looked smoky and murky.

"The air here is so much cleaner. I guess that makes a difference."

25

He took her elbow to keep her from stumbling on a crack in the pavement, and she said in what she hoped was a lady-like tone, "Thank you. I guess I'd better look where I'm going instead of at the stars."

"Oh, that's okay. Do you know how to find the Little Dipper?" he asked her, still holding her elbow.

"No, do you?" She looked at him in surprise. "You find the North Star first, which is one of the biggest, brightest stars directly overhead." He let go of her to indicate a bright star located almost true north. "That's Polaris, or the North Star." By this time they had stopped, and were both gazing up into the night sky. "There's a Big Dipper and a Little Dipper, you know," he told her, looking at her as he spoke.

"I remember studying a little about them in school, but I don't remember much except their Latin names, Ursa Major and Ursa Minor, which means Big Bear and Little Bear," she commented. "The Big and Little Dipper are both star groups in the constellations Big Bear and Little Bear, but I never learned how to locate them."

"To find the Big Dipper, you have to locate the Little Dipper first. The handle of the Big Dipper points to Polaris, which is the last star in the handle of the Little Dipper, so when you find one you can usually find the other. See them right up there?" he asked, taking her hand and using her index finger to point to them.

"Oh, yes, I see them!" She looked to where they pointed together, his hand guiding her finger. "How did you know all that?" she asked, looking at him and suddenly realizing that his left hand lay on her left shoulder, as both their right hands were pointed toward the stars.

"My dad. He knows a lot about the different constellations and the stars that are located in them." He cleared his throat before speaking, "I guess I'd better get you home before your brother starts to wondering where we are." Sarah felt like she'd been a long way in the short while they'd been gone. It seemed strange to be walking into the familiar front yard with the porch light shining.

Suddenly a figure sitting on the steps caught her eye. It was Peter! He'd waited up for her!

"Hello, Sarah. Charlie. Did you enjoy the movie? It was such a nice evening I wanted to sit outside and enjoy it." "It is nice, and it was a good movie, too," responded Sarah, flattered that Peter had waited up for her.

"Yeah, it was a great movie."

"Charlie showed me the Big and Little Dippers, Peter. His dad showed them to him," she said, looking up at Charlie as if he were the smartest boy in the world.

"Oh, that—that was nice," Peter said heartily, looking from one to the other. For some reason his manner made Sarah feel a little embarrassed and guilty, as if he thought they'd done something wrong. An unexpected trickle of resentment entered her stomach, reminiscent of Friday night. *How on earth did they expect her to know how to act, and yet still have a good time?*

"Well, I guess I'd better go," Charlie said quickly, looking from Peter to Sarah. Sarah's mind flashed to the incident when he'd had his arm around her, and flushed in embarrassment.

"Thanks for the company. I'll see you later, Sarah. You, too, Preacher." He nodded at Peter and turned to cross the road to his house. Peter and Sarah went around to the back door. She wistfully glanced over her shoulder as she closed the door behind her.

The next day was Sunday and Peter held services at West Bend Church. The church building appeared to be older than the Ulcanush Church and designed more simply. Sarah thought the members appeared to be less blessed materially, and more reserved. She hoped she would get to know them better at the vacation Bible school beginning the next day. Peter and Lois arrived at 8:30 to enroll the students as the first order of business. Peter asked Sarah to help with the registration. She took pencils and enrollment cards to the designated classes, beginning with the class for four and five-year olds. Their mothers accompanied the children to their class so Sarah asked them to complete the cards. Then she asked some additional questions.

"What is his/her full name? Date of birth?" She noticed immediately an air of reserve and a reluctance to answer her questions. She felt it was due to shyness, since she was a stranger to them and so she persevered, trying to be as warm and yet respectful as she could. It took quite a while to enroll all the students but eventually the task was complete. Sarah felt a sense of accomplishment that she was able to help.

Peter and Lois took an active part in assisting with the lessons. They worked outside on picnic tables under the shade of large oak trees. The children worked with interest and enthusiasm, proud of each project they completed. Many wore their enthusiasm with splashes of tempera paint on their hands, faces, and clothes. They were all so excited to use the art supplies and create their own masterpieces.

Cookies and Kool-Aid were always a welcome part of the morning. Soon Friday rolled around. The school commencement was scheduled for that evening for the parents to receive a firsthand knowledge of their children's lessons. Each class teacher gave a short synopsis of the Bible lessons and activities, and then the parents viewed the handwork displays set up on tables in the wide downstairs hallway. Again refreshments of sandwiches, chips, cookies, cup cakes and punch were served. Most of the children took their food and drink outside to the picnic tables while their parents chatted among themselves and the teachers.

During the commencement exercises, Peter came to Sarah and asked her to fill in with the four and five-year old class, whose teacher was unable to be present. Sarah was to lead the children to the choir area, and help them sing the simple songs they had learned during the week. It frightened her to be responsible for the children on such short notice, but she felt obligated to accept. She was familiar with the songs, which she'd learned herself as a child: "Praise Him All Ye little Children," "Jesus Loves Me," and "The B-I-B-L-E." The children stumbled over some of the words, but the pianist and the music leader helped Sarah get them through it.

The song leader was a blonde young man in his middle to late twenties, of whom Sarah stood in awe. He was very nice looking and was music director for the church. He stood behind the pianist and directed the children as they sang. Sarah fastened her gaze on top of the piano for the first couple of songs. *If I don't look at him I'll be all right*. It unnerved her to see all those faces looking in her direction, and then in spite of her resolve to not look at the music leader, her eyes were drawn to him. She felt paralyzed by her stage fright and self-consciousness. At last she was able to lead the children from the choir loft to sit with their parents. Her cheeks burned with embarrassment. She felt like such a failure. Peter thanked her, however, and seemed satisfied with her efforts.

The next week the Bible school was held in the evenings at Ulcanush. Charlie Cotton drove his father's old red pickup truck to pick up children who needed transportation. Peter rode with him up front, and the children stood up in the back and held on to the sides of the wooden homemade body. They enjoyed the ride, and sang, talked, laughed, and poked fun at each other, as children will do. Sarah stood towards the front next to the cab of the truck. She especially enjoyed the trip home after the school was over, because then it was dark and she could look up at the night sky to see the stars, and feel the wind blowing through her hair.

Learning the books of the Bible was the emphasis for the older children during the week. Sarah had learned many of them in previous years of Bible school attendance, but her memory grew shaky of the Old Testament books after Amos, and after Colossians in the New Testament. Her favorite books in the Old Testament were Ruth and Esther.

During the commencement exercises the children who had learned the books of either the Old or New Testaments were given an opportunity to recite them. One rather stout teenaged girl quoted the books of the Old Testament, incorrectly pronouncing the books that ended in the "a" sound, using the "er" sound instead, but she was earnest about it, and her enthusiasm for the Scriptures made up for errors in pronouncement. Peter stressed the importance of learning the books of the Bible after the students had finished their recitations, stating that this knowledge would stay with the children for the rest of their lives. The younger children had learned simple Bible verses, and he praised all those who were able to remember a verse learned that week. He thanked all the teachers who had worked in the Bible School, those who had helped serve the refreshments, and Charlie Cotton for bringing the children back and forth to the church each evening.

Soon it was time for the church revivals. Peter preached and the music was especially heartwarming and stirring. Sarah received a blessing at both revivals, and was thrilled when those who made commitments to God came forward, whether it was to accept Christ as their personal Savior, or for rededication of their lives.

Charlie Cotton attended the revival services at Ulcanush Church and he asked Peter and Lois if he could bring Sarah home. They gave their permission without hesitation. Sarah felt they now had more confidence in both of them after getting to know Charlie better. His help transporting the children to and fro did not go unnoticed. Since Peter and he rode together in the cab of the truck, they had an opportunity to talk and fellowship with one another and had become friends. Sarah was surprised and pleased when Charlie came up to her after the first night's service and asked if she'd like to ride home with him in the old red pickup truck. It could have been a Cadillac for all the difference it made to her.

"Would you mind if I take you home?" he'd asked her, his hair combed carefully and smoothed down with hair tonic.

"I'd be honored."

They walked together to the truck, and he opened her door so that she could climb in. It was a bit of a step up, but she managed to get in without too much difficulty and with as much modesty as possible. Charlie climbed into the driver's seat and revved up the truck's motor. Soon they were riding through the night with the engine roaring and the wind blowing through the open windows, forcing them to speak loudly to each other in order to be heard.

"What grade will you be in this year?" asked Charlie.

"The tenth. What grade will you be in?"

"I'll be in the eleventh. What are your best subjects?"

"I like English, History, and Biology. We are required to take Biology at my school. Is it required at yours?"

"No, we're just a small, country school and not many students go on to college."

"I'd like to go to college, if I can. It costs a lot of money, though."

"Yeah, it sure does."

"What are your hobbies? What do you enjoy doing?" she asked. They were coming through town now and weren't far from her house.

"Oh, I like to swim, and go fishing, play a little baseball. What about you?"

"I enjoy reading and drawing, but I'm afraid that I'm not very athletic," she replied, smiling at him with a rueful expression.

"May I bring you home tomorrow night, if it's okay with your folks?"

By this time he was pulling up in front of her house. The lights were on so someone was home.

"Yes, I'd like that."

She smiled at him as she started to open the door then suddenly stopped herself. She remembered that the girl is supposed to wait for the boy to open her car door. He came around the truck and opened her door, and she stepped down. He had to assist her, for she almost stumbled as she stepped onto the ground.

"Tomorrow night, then. Good night," he called as he rounded the front of the truck.

"Yes, good night," she called in return, and began walking to the door of the house. When she stepped inside, only a small lamp burned in the living room. She noticed another light and followed into the kitchen. Peter and Lois were seated at the table with a glass of milk each. They were eating peanut butter and saltine crackers, Peter's favorite nighttime snack.

"Care to join us?" he asked her.

"I think I'll just have some milk." She reached into the cabinet for a glass. Lois spoke up as Sarah poured milk into her glass.

"Is he going to bring you home tomorrow night?"

"He said he would if it was all right with you all," she answered, looking from Peter to Lois inquiringly.

"It's fine with me if he brings you home every night," Peter said.

"Yes, he seems to be a pretty nice boy," agreed Lois, draining her glass.

"Well, okay—thanks."

She smiled. She, too, finished her milk, and taking Lois and Peter's glasses with hers to the water bucket, she poured a small amount into their glasses to keep from leaving a ring in them.

"See you for devotions?" asked Peter, leaning his head around the doorframe toward her.

"Sure. Just give me a few minutes."

."Okay, see you then."

Sarah rinsed out her mouth, and put up the crackers and peanut butter. Then she went into her room to put on her gown and housecoat. Peter and Lois had been coming into her room for devotions during the revivals, to keep from waking Kelly, who was usually asleep by this time every evening.

Charlie continued to bring Sarah home each evening. They were becoming better acquainted, and Sarah felt more relaxed and comfortable with him. She was able to keep up her end of the conversation, and she laughed readily at his attempts at humor.

"Say, have you been able to see much of the place since you've been here—like the river?" he asked. "That and the creeks are the only place we have to go swimming around here."

"No, I haven't seen much. Just the post office and the general store."

"Would you like to go for a drive tomorrow? I can show you the river. It's not far from here."

"Oh, yes, I'd like to see it. And more of the country side, too."

"How about I pick you up around three o'clock. I'll ask your folks tonight if it'll be okay."

"Sounds great. I didn't bring a bathing suit, but I can't swim anyway."

"Oh, that's okay. We can get out and walk around some, take our shoes off if we want."

They had reached her house, and she waited inside the truck for him to come around to open her door. This time she made a more graceful exit. When they entered the living room Sarah saw that

Peter and Lois were once again in the kitchen so she and Charlie went on back to join them.

"Good evening, Charlie. How about a piece of cake and a glass of milk?" Lois offered.

"Yes, ma'am. That'd be nice," he replied, as Sarah went to the cabinet to get glasses, and saucers for the cake.

"Oh, you made chocolate pound cake!" exclaimed Sarah. "You'll love her chocolate pound cake. It's delicious."

She cut them each a slice and poured their milk, then gave Charlie a napkin and fork.

"It sure looks good," he said, looking at it appreciatively. They began eating, and after Charlie had swallowed his first bite, he cleared his throat and asked Peter, "Would it be all right if I took Sarah for a look at some of our countryside and to see the river?"

"Oh, I think that could be arranged, don't you think?" Peter answered, as he turned to get Lois's approval.

"Tomorrow evening, you mean?" he asked Charlie.

"Yes, sir."

"Yes, I suppose. What time will you pick her up?"

"Around three o'clock. I thought that would get us home in time to eat supper and get ready for church," he said around another bite of cake.

"Yes, that should be all right," agreed Lois.

They finished up their dessert, and Charlie rose and pushed his chair under the table.

"Thanks for the cake. It was very good."

"Oh, I'm just glad you enjoyed it," Lois acknowledged, a satisfied smile on her face.

"I'll walk you to the door," Sarah offered, as she turned to accompany him to the living room.

"Good night, Preacher, Miss Lois," he said, turning around at the kitchen door.

"Good night, Charlie. Come again." They reached the front door, and Sarah held the screen door open as she leaned out to wish him good night.

"See you tomorrow afternoon, then," Charlie told Sarah.

She nodded her head in reply, and called softly so as not to wake up Kelly, "Good night." Charlie turned to wave before getting into his truck.

The next afternoon Charlie picked Sarah up promptly at three o'clock and drove out onto some of the side roads around the town. Peter and Lois were kept busy with the two churches and had not had a chance to take her to sightsee. One road pretty much looked like another to Sarah.

During the revival at West Bend Church the pastor and his family had been invited out for supper every evening before church. The average home they'd entered was unpainted on the exterior and simply furnished inside. They had been welcomed, somewhat shyly at times but graciously. Meals of fried chicken, skinned before frying and browned to a crisp hardness, Crowder peas or butter beans, potato salad, sliced tomatoes, bread, and tea were the usual fare.

It was interesting to see the different homes, walk on the often worn linoleum floors, eat in the kitchen rather than the dining room, and to see that poverty dwelt in many a household. It was along roads like these that Charlie drove her.

The only luxurious home to which the pastor's family had visited had been Grey Fleming's home. He led the music during the vacation Bible school at West Bend Church. Mrs. Fleming had a beautiful home with full-sized dining room and a sheltered patio outside. She had served a delicious meal of baked ham, tomato aspic salad, hot homemade rolls, asparagus casserole, iced tea, and pecan pie topped with ice cream.

Finally, after naming every family whose house they'd passed, Charlie asked her if she was thirsty and wanted a cola.

"That'd taste good," she answered him, with an appreciative smile.

The roads were dry and dusty, the afternoon hot without a sign of a breeze. Her mouth and throat felt dry. He pulled up in front of a greasy spoon and they went inside. The jukebox was playing country music and the restaurant smelled of fried potatoes and onions. He bought them two bottles of cola and they took them back to the truck. After driving a short distance he parked the truck.

"Want to walk a little?" he asked her.

She had worn her brown sandals, which were not made for walking much distance, but she was tired of bumping along the dry roads.

"I guess so. How far will we walk?"

"Oh, not very far. I've got a surprise for you," he smiled mysteriously.

"Really? That sounds interesting!"

He opened her door, and she climbed nimbly out (she'd gotten the hang of it now) and stepped down to the ground.

They began walking and the hot sun beat down on their heads, but the ice-cold colas helped to wash the dust from their mouths. The road was rock and sand, and grit began to sift into her sandals, but she trudged valiantly on. His cowboy boots offered him excellent protection, she noted enviously.

Soon the road began to slant downhill and she glimpsed a line of trees in the distance. As they got closer she saw the trees lined a wide expanse of muddy-looking water.

"Is this the famous river?" she teased him, wiping the sweat from her eyes so she could see better, and holding the cold cola bottle to her forehead. As they drew close enough to stand on its bank, she asked doubtfully, "This is where you go swimming?"

"Yep. It's not too deep along here, just up to your waist. It gets up to your chest toward the middle though," Charlie explained.

"What did you say its name was?" she asked him, squinting up at him, her nose wrinkling.

"The Tombigbee."

"That sounds like an Indian name."

She looked thoughtfully at the muddy water.

"It is. It and the Alabama rivers join together near Mobile and make up the Mobile River, which empties into the Mobile Bay."

"Mobile is on the coast, then, isn't it? Have you ever been there?"

"Yeah, a few times. It's pretty."

"Is Alabama an Indian name, too?"

"Yes. It got its name from an Indian tribe who lived here before the white man, only they spelled it, Alibamu," he told her.

"Boy, you know your history," she complimented him.

"Say, I'll bet Ulcanush is an Indian name, too, isn't it?"

"Yes, it is. And yes, I do like history."

He smiled at her surprise that he enjoyed history. "Actually, several more rivers have Indian names, and also counties and towns. The Indian names have a musical sound, I think, and aren't really that hard to pronounce. Like Tuscaloosa, Choctaw, Etowah, Conecuh, Leohatchee, Tallapoosa, Tallassee, Tecumseh, Wedowee, Chicasaw, and Cherokee," he continued.

"Oh, and some of the names are of actual Indian tribes, like Choctaw, Chicasaw, and Cherokee, aren't they? I suppose they once lived around here, too," Sarah commented thoughtfully. "I always found the Indians fascinating."

"Oh, so you find me fascinating?" he teased.

"Are you part Indian?" she questioned, looking closely into his face.

"My great-great grandmother was full-blooded Cherokee. I guess that's why I enjoy learning about them. The Indians made a great contribution to our country, and left their names for many of the states from east to west."

"That is true, isn't it? Connecticut, North and South Dakota, Minnesota, Mississippi. Illinois, Wyoming, Oklahoma, Iowa, and Illinois, just to name some," she mused, looking across the river to the opposite shore.

He felt a connection between them, so he stepped close and put his arm around her and squeezed her shoulder lightly. She didn't pull away from him but looked up, smiling into his face.

"I really enjoyed this afternoon," she told him.

He squeezed her shoulder again, and after a final look at the river, they turned to go. His hand slipped down her arm and took her hand as they began their walk back to the truck. Sarah never dreamed that this would be one of their last times together.

When she and Charlie returned to the parsonage, Lois met them at the front door. Sarah knew from Lois's expression that something was wrong.

They went in and Lois said to Sarah, "I'm so glad you got back a little early. Your mother called. She's scheduled for surgery day after tomorrow morning. It's her gall bladder. She needs you to come home to stay with her when it's over."

"She's in the hospital now?" Sarah asked anxiously.

"Yes. They just admitted her about an hour ago. They've got to do some blood work, and start her on antibiotics. They say her gall bladder is enlarged. They don't want it to rupture," Lois explained, taking Sarah's hand to reassure her.

Peter came into the room just then, and told Sarah, "I've checked on the bus schedules and you can catch one leaving at nine o'clock tonight. That would be better, anyway, so you can get some sleep and arrive in Greenville around eight o'clock in the morning. You'll go straight through, no changes or stopovers, and you can take a cab home from the bus station in Greenville. Then you can take a city bus to and from the hospital. Do you have any money?"

"Yes, I've got about $21.00. Will that be enough?"

"Well, that's enough to buy your bus ticket to Greenville, but I'm going to let you have another $15.00 for your eats and any other expenses," Peter said, putting his arm around her to comfort her.

"Mother's never had a gall bladder attack in her life. Is it serious?"

"The doctor thinks she has only one large stone but they need to run more tests," Lois told her.

"Gosh, Sarah, I'm sure sorry about your mother. I hope she's going to be okay," Charlie said sympathetically.

"Thanks, Charlie. This is such a shock! I don't know what to say. I guess I'll have to get my suitcase and start packing. Can he stay and eat supper?" she asked Lois, and looked questioningly at Peter.

"Yes, I've already got something ready. We'll eat now and then you can pack. Peter can drive you to the bus station in Grove Hill— oh, but he's got the revival..." Lois paused, looking at Peter.

"I'll take her, if that's okay. I've got a full tank of gas and it'll give us a chance to say goodbye." Charlie offered.

Sarah turned to look at him gratefully. Her eyes misted with worry for her mother, and disappointment to be leaving so soon, before the summer was over. Even though there were only a couple of weeks left before school started, she'd planned on staying until the last week of summer.

"I'd better call Kelly in to eat." Lois went to the back door to call her in for supper.

"You're welcome to stay and eat with us, Charlie. And I really appreciate your doing this. It's really a life saver for us," Peter said, taking Charlie's hand in a firm handshake.

"Oh, I'm just glad I can do something to help," Charlie told him. "I'd better go let the folks know what's happening," he said apologetically. "I'll be back in a few minutes."

"That'll be fine. It'll give me time to set the table and put the food on," Lois said, as she and Sarah walked him part way to the door.

Just then Kelly came in, her eyes big and out of breath from running. "Sarah, do you really hafta go?" she asked, her eyes beginning to tear up.

"Yes, sweetheart, I do. Mother's very sick, and has to have an operation. I've got to go home to help take care of her when she comes home from the hospital." Sarah got on her knees to hug the child closely to her.

"What's an op—opera-shun?" Kelly asked.

"Well, she has a sick gall bladder, something in her stomach, that the doctors have to take out to make her well," explained Sarah.

"Oh—I've never been to the hospital, have I?" she asked, looking up at her mother.

"No, except when you were born," answered Lois, smiling and ruffling Kelly's blonde curls.

Charlie returned then, and they went into the kitchen to eat. Sarah helped Lois to make quick work of the dishes and than began packing her suitcase.

Peter and Charlie took Kelly outside with them to check the oil in Charlie's truck. All too soon it was time to go. Sarah hugged Peter, and Lois, and Kelly once more, in farewell.

"I've enjoyed the summer so very much, and appreciate your inviting me," she told them.

"Call us and let us know how Mother gets along, and tell her that as soon as the revival is over, we'll come for a good visit," requested Peter.

"I will. She'll be glad to hear that."

Charlie took Sarah's suitcase to the truck and put it in the back.

"Tell everybody goodbye for me," called Sarah, before turning to get into the truck. She waved as they started off, and looked back at them once more until they were out of sight.

Charlie and Sarah were silent for a few moments, their thoughts and feelings mixed. Both felt a sadness of having her visit cut short, concern for the sick mother in the hospital, and the realization that this was goodbye.

"Greenville has a good hospital and very good doctors," said Sarah, as if trying to reassure herself.

"Oh, that's good. I'm sure your mother will be fine. My grandmother had hers out last year and did great, and she's sixty-five."

"Sarah, I want to say how much I've enjoyed getting to know you this summer. You're different from any girl I've ever known, and I'll always remember you."

"Thank you, Charlie. That means a lot to me. I've enjoyed knowing you, too, and I hope you'll write me."

"I'll write you first, and give you my address," he promised, laying his hand over hers on the seat. Before they were ready, the bus station came into view. Charlie parked at the curb, and got out to get her suitcase and to open her door. They heard the bus driver announce the destinations as he stood by the bus to await his passengers. Sarah hurried to get her ticket, but no one was ahead of her at the ticket window so it only took a few minutes.

Charlie gave her suitcase to the bus driver for loading into the baggage hold. She approached Charlie and then, as if they had the same thought, she reached to hug him around the neck, and he closed his arms tightly around her for just a minute before she turned away to step into the bus.

The bus driver started his engine, and Sarah waved at him as they pulled out of the station. She watched him as long as she could, as he did her, with a last wave of farewell.

"It had been an eventful summer," Sarah thought in retrospect. One she'd always remember.

She'd learned a lot and had grown a lot. *And Charlie had promised to write.*

She sighed and leaned her head back against the seat as the bus began to start the long drive home.

THE RIDE

It began as an ordinary trip to the mountains, which were clad in a glorious riot of autumn colors. The weather was ideal for early October. Fluffy white clouds floated in an azure sky, and there was just a hint of crispness in the air. The leaves, ranging from brilliant gold to deep magenta, contrasted starkly with the dark green pines and the deep blue of the distant mountains, a picturesque display at each bend of the winding road.

Jean drove her Ford sedan, still dependable, but showing its age in the fading paint and worn seat covers. Seventeen-year-old twins Megan and Melissa Jones and their older sister, Betty, enjoyed Jean's company. She was an easy-going woman close to fifty who had taken the parentless girls under her wing (their father dead, and their mother confined to a mental hospital). They enjoyed the many outings on which she invited them. Megan and Melissa shared the usual close bond that exists between identical twins, went everywhere together, and were in the same classes at school.

There was the usual personality difference, as in all identical twins, and because they looked alike they confused their teachers.

"How much farther is it to the Indian reservation?" asked Megan.

"Oh, we should be there before too long. Getting hungry?" replied Jean.

Her gray eyes twinkled behind the dark-framed glasses.

"The fried chicken and the potato salad smell very appetizing," laughed Megan, who had been sniffing at the food basket sitting next to her in the back seat for the past hour.

They decided to stop for a brief lunch and Jean pulled off to a roadside park. Soon they were enjoying the delicacies—fried chicken, potato salad, pimento cheese sandwiches, cokes, and chocolate cake. "We've brought so much food there's plenty left for supper," declared Betty, the twins' older sister, as they packed up the leftovers, all having eaten until they were full.

Once on the road again, Jean asked Megan and Melissa to sing some of the current popular songs. The girls' soprano voices blended with the hum of the tires as they rode through the spectacular scenery around them—deep valleys amidst hills clad in the fall-colored trees.

Before long, they reached their destination, Cherokee, N. C., the site of the Cherokee Indian Reservation. Megan and Melissa gazed in fascination at the souvenir shops that lined both sides of the streets, and at the mobs of people everywhere they looked. Jean had to slow down to a crawl to avoid the pedestrians, and eased into the lone parking space that was left. She parked the car, locked it, then led the way.

As they entered each shop they found it thronged with shoppers. It was impossible to linger long at any display due to the crush of people behind them, so they had to move along, trying to avoid the souvenir seekers around them. They were constantly bumping into someone, or someone would bump into them and were so busy saying, "excuse me," they were unable to see all of the things they would have liked. They weaved in and out among the people as best they could in order to pick up an object to observe it more in detail. Soon they gave it up as too difficult a task.

To compound the problem, most of the shops were small. Fortunately, others were larger and less crowded and they could move leisurely, look and examine items more closely before deciding if they wished to buy them.

There were ashtrays, mugs, fake tomahawks, lamps, rugs, and bedspreads for sale. As is often the case in many souvenir shops, most of the items were either cheaply made or gaudy with garish colors, others distasteful to the point of vulgarity. The smells were of closely packed humanity, varying from aromas of onion breaths, body odors, and loud perfumes.

After a couple of hours they were tired, and agreed that they had seen enough, as all the wares were more or less the same in every shop.

Leaving the shops with their purchases they were fortunate to meet a Cherokee Chief on the sidewalk. Jean asked the Chief for his permission to have the girls' pictures taken with him and he graciously agreed. Jean soon had them posed as a group and snapped several pictures of them.

"Boy, that'll be something to show the kids at school, won't it?" Jean laughed, digging her elbow into Megan's ribs.

"You bet!" Megan grinned.

It was late afternoon, and shadows were beginning to fall, and since they were hungry again, they stopped at another park to polish off the leftovers before heading back home. As they were eating, Jean asked, "Do you girls mind if I stop to see my old friends, Jim and Maggie Goodwin? I haven't seen them in a month of Sundays."

The girls couldn't object since they were Jean's guests and she was driving.

They packed up their things and got back on the road again. Turning onto a side road off the main highway, they soon found themselves on a winding graveled road that led into more thickly wooded terrain. Finally Jean pulled into the yard of a clapboard house near the road and honked her horn.

A light through the windows revealed that someone was home. A tall, slim man opened the screen door and peered into the darkness, closely followed by the short, plump figure of his wife. Recognizing Jean after looking closely at the car, the man stepped down off the porch. His wife, Maggie, had recognized Jean at once, and rushed ahead of her husband to grab her around the neck.

"Why, Jean Thompson, come in and stay awhile. It's been a long time since we've seen the likes of you. What are you doing in this neck of the woods?" she exclaimed.

Everyone piled out of the car and followed the couple into the simply furnished, though comfortable front room. Jean introduced the girls, who shook hands with the couple's, and everyone sat down on chairs or on the long sofa. Jean and the Goodwins chatted for a few minutes, catching up on news of each other amid friendly teasing on both sides with much laughter. Finally, Jean asked Jim if he'd done much fishing lately.

"Well, as it so happens I'd planned to meet Tom Manly at his house early tomorrow morning for a day of it, but my old pickup's on the blink. Sure hate for him to drive all the way up here to pick me up, then have to turn right around to bring me home tomorrow night," he replied.

"How far from here does he live?" Jean asked.

"Oh, it's about eight to ten miles; the road's in pretty good shape, just has a few bumps and crooked as a snake to boot." Having lived in these backwoods all his life, he considered it better than some, which were hardly fit to travel, especially in winter, for being this high up they received snow and ice; then they were, indeed, unsafe for travel.

"Why don't you let us run you down to Tom's house since we're going that way? Won't be but a hop, skip, and jump, once we get back on the main road. Come morning you can get an early start on your fishing. Maybe when Tom brings you home he can take a look at your old clunker at the same time. He's a good mechanic, isn't he?" offered Jean.

"Well, sure, he's the best but I hate to put you out," Jim had the typical mountain man's aversion to being a bother and possessed the strong self-reliance typical of his breed.

"Oh, we don't mind a bit. Get your gear and put it in the trunk, and we'll get started. Here, take the trunk key and load up while I say a few more words to Maggie," Jean directed.

Jim stowed his gear in the trunk and they were ready to leave. Megan brought up the rear. Jean took the wheel, leaving Megan no choice but to sit between Jim Goodwin and Jean.

"Turn right at the next road," Jim said.

Megan was surprised at how close his voice sounded. She glanced around to find that he had casually draped his arm over the back of the seat as he'd settled in. She told herself that it simply was because of being in the small car with three people sharing the front seat. As it was, Jean had just enough room to shift gears.

The road was, indeed, crooked as a snake. As much as Megan tried to sit up straight the gravitational pull of the car as it rounded the road's curves made it impossible. Despite her best efforts, she would slide on the smooth seat onto Jim Goodwin's side as they went around a curve, helpless to move back until the car had straightened out. It seemed as if he'd moved fractionally closer to her, for she was almost touching the arm that he'd draped behind her over the back of the seat.

Jim and Jean talked over her head, and she wondered if he were even aware of their close proximity. She began to feel the pressure of his thigh against hers as they rounded another turn in the road. In the quiet darkness of the car, punctuated only by an occasional comment or two, she soon found herself relaxing, letting the movement of the car carry her, and ceasing her useless struggle to keep her body from touching his. Jim had moved closer, and now she sat within the curve of his shoulder.

She began to enjoy the feel of his firm thigh against hers, and the intimate contact against his ribs and chest as she was swung against his warmth on the curves of the winding road. Their pleasant physical closeness and the hum of the motor had a hypnotic effect on her. It seemed as though they had been riding for hours in the intimate darkness.

Rather than tensing away from him as before, Megan now leaned into him, letting her softness remain against his hardness until the car swung her away from him, much like a rider would sway in the saddle as he rose and fell in one motion with his horse.

Almost in a trance, Megan didn't see the lights that shone in the darkness ahead and she was half-startled when Jean stopped in front of a house. Jean removed the key from the ignition and opened the door. As she got out to open the trunk, Jim climbed out also. Megan heard them talking together as he removed his fishing gear.

Then he and Jean said their farewells, and Jim stepped onto the porch to go inside his friend's house. As Jean opened her door and the inside lights came on, Megan turned her head so that Jim couldn't see her face.

Jean started up the car and they began to drive toward home. Megan heard Betty ask Jean and Melissa as the car began to pick up speed, "He had his arm around Megan, didn't he?"

Megan said nothing and neither did the others, as if were of no importance.

Megan knew it had been important to her, however, because she had felt a new self-awareness, almost a new identity. She would keep the experience to herself, not sharing it with anyone. It was too personal, belonging only to herself. She would tuck it away for safe keeping, knowing she'd grown–had changed somehow–for she'd just been given an understanding of the woman she would become.

NEW BEGINNINGS

The year was 1952, seven years after the end of World War II. The setting was Greenville, South Carolina, the heart of the textile industry.

"Ella, there's a secretarial job open at Economy Textiles," Ella's older sister, Doris, informed her.

"Economy Textiles? Where's that?"

"You know, it's right across the road from the G & N Railroad where I work. My boss told me about it."

"Oh, yes. Well, at least that'll be easy for me to find. Thanks!"

Ella had just finished high school and needed a job. She was glad Doris had told her it was available. She knew she had no choice but to apply. She'd have to work for a living now.

"I'll check into it today. Let me see…today's Thursday, isn't it? They might let me start work on Monday, that is if I get it."

Ella felt both doubtful and hopeful about applying for the job. Her expression reflected her mixed feelings.

"They may have other applications to consider. Don't get your hopes up too high, just in case."

Ella dressed carefully to present a neat appearance. Her shorthand and typing teacher had instructed the class how to dress for an interview. She'd given them many helpful pointers, from how many erasures a letter was allowed and the number of words per minute a secretary should be able to type, to the words per minute she was expected to write shorthand, and how to be professional on the job.

She caught a bus and got off at the stop nearest her destination, about a block and a half away. As she walked, she noticed the greasy spoon restaurant, rundown hotel, and beer parlor across the street. The street received its name, River Street, from the Reedy River nearby.

The river was polluted from the wastes that local industries dumped into its water, giving it an unpleasant odor. The bridge, which spanned the river, was just past where she could turn to arrive at Economy Textiles. The G & N Railroad was about a block down on the left.

With heart beating in trepidation, Ella turned into the yard of the low, white building surrounded by a chain link fence. She continued on to the front steps and knocked. The door immediately opened and she looked up into the rather prominent features of a tall, gray-haired man, who looked to be in his mid-to-late fifties.

"Hello, you must be Ella. I knew your voice sounded young on the phone, but you don't look old enough to be out of school, much less on your own looking for a job."

He reached out to shake her hand, her small hand becoming enveloped in his large one.

"I just finished high school the first week in June, and won't be eighteen until August 17th."

"Come on into my office and we'll discuss your qualifications. I'm Frank N. Quinn. Won't you have a seat?"

"Thank you."

Ella sat down in the seat opposite Mr. Quinn and clasped her hands together on the desk to hide their trembling.

"We need someone who can take shorthand and type. You said you had taken a business course in high school. How many words a minute can you type?"

"Fifty."

Ella had added a little to her usual speed of forty-two words per minute. Her typing teacher had despaired her ever learning to type, although she'd made excellent grades in shorthand.

"And how many words per minute do you take shorthand from dictation?"

"Sixty."

Ella had stretched her shorthand ability just a bit as well. Her shorthand teacher had told her class that some jobs, such as a court stenographer, required 120 words per minute. The average boss, however, did not dictate more than sixty to eighty words per minute, most even less. She just had to get this job to help out at home. To fail would cause censure and reproach from her sister.

"That sounds very good. We need another girl in the office to do letters. We have only two secretaries right now. They simply cannot handle all the correspondence and do their other tasks as well. Could you start, say, on Monday morning at eight o'clock?"

"Yes, sir."

"Fine, fine. Our hours are from eight to five. You'll have a time card which you'll punch every morning, when you leave for lunch and return, and again when you leave in the afternoon. The pay is one dollar an hour less taxes. Does that sound satisfactory?"

"Yes, sir. That sounds fine."

"Good, good. We'll look for you on Monday morning then. We have a coffee break in the morning, and a break in the afternoon."

Ella noticed he often repeated himself and he spoke with a slow drawl. She couldn't place it then, but she was to learn later that he'd been raised in a children's home in Florida.

Just then Frankie Styles, one of the other secretaries, knocked on Mr. Quinn's office door. She cracked the door wide enough to permit her to look inside. Mr. Quinn rose immediately and motioned for her to come in.

"Frankie, I didn't know you were back from the bank. Come in, come in."

"Frankie Styles meet Ella Raines. She's applying for the secretarial position. Frankie, would you show her around and explain what she'll be doing?"

"Yes, sir. Don't forget you're to meet your wife for lunch at eleven-thirty."

"Oh, that's right. It had already slipped my mind."

He looked at Ella and then Frankie and smiled.

"Now you see why I need someone around to keep me straight, Ella."

Ella smiled back at the two of them and then followed Frankie out of Mr. Quinn's office.

Frankie was a habitual gum chewer. She chewed gum as some people chew tobacco or dip snuff. Her jaws moved constantly, and not only did she rapidly chew her gum, but she popped it regularly as well.

As Frankie began to explain what her duties would be, Ella's attention was drawn more to her voice than what she was saying.

She has a country twang. I'll bet she lives above Greenville, close to the mountains.

She quickly brought her attention back to what Frankie was instructing her to do.

"You'll have to order the greige goods for Stone Manufacturing Company according to their schedule. It's in their customer file folders. Just thumb through each one until you find it. It'll be on a yellow carbon copy sheet."

Ella was a little bewildered by Frankie's explanations since she'd let her attention wander for a minute.

Maybe I can figure it out later or I'll ask Frankie again.

Frankie's hair was upswept in front and pulled into a knot at the back. Tendrils escaped to hang down in the back. Tiny freckles dotted her complexion, and the deep pink of her lipstick was becoming.

Frankie looked over Ella's appearance as she talked, and Ella felt that she was estimating how much her outfit was worth. Her manner was casual, but Ella got the impression that the wheels in Frankie's brain were always turning, allowing her to quickly adjust from one subject to another without losing her train of thought. Her blue eyes and dark blonde hair suited both her complexion and her personality.

They seated themselves to go over the files. Frankie sat at her desk across from Mr. Quinn's office door and Ella automatically took the next desk, but had to roll her chair over to see the files that Frankie was going over with her.

"Billie Long is Mr. Quinn's secretary. She does the bookkeeping. Her desk is in Mr. Quinn's office, but she's at lunch right now. She should be back soon."

Despite the fact that Frankie was obviously in her twenties, she had something in the timbre of her voice and manner of speaking that reminded Ella of an old country woman whose voice was beginning to get high.

"It's time for me to go to lunch. If the phone rings, you can answer it until Billie gets back. Her full name is Willie Mae Long, but everybody calls her Billie."

"Okay. Just answer Economy Textiles?"

"Yes, and if there's a message for Mr. Quinn or a number for him to call, just write them down on this pink pad."

Ella took the pink pad and pen from Frankie's desk and sat down at her own. There wasn't a phone on her desk, but she needed only to roll her chair over to Frankie's to take the calls. There were three separate lines; one for Mr. Quinn's office, one for Frankie's desk, and the third one for the warehouse.

Ella glanced into Mr. Quinn's office. He hadn't returned from lunch, so she was left to handle any phone calls until Billie came in. It seemed she would go to lunch last. She picked up several files on Frankie's desk to see if she could familiarize herself with some of the routine correspondence, shipments, and invoices. It all looked pretty much like Greek to her, but she was able to learn some of the workings of the plant. It was all rather confusing, but she hoped to catch on to the work soon and be able to do what was expected of her.

Suddenly the phone rang. She rolled over to Frankie's desk and picked up the receiver.

"Hello, this is Economy Textiles." She'd almost forgotten, in her excitement, how to answer. Her hand was damp on the receiver.

"Mr. Frank Quinn, please."

"I'm sorry but he's out to lunch. He should be back shortly. May I take a message or have him return your call?"

"Yes. Please have him call Eugene Stone, III, of Stone Manufacturing Company. He knows my number."

"Certainly, Mr. Stone. I'll leave the message on his desk."

"I don't recognize your voice, Miss. With whom am I speaking?"

"Ella Raines. This is my first day here."

"Well, Ella, I hope you have a long and successful tenure with Economy Textiles."

"Thank you, Mr. Stone."

As they ended the conversation, another girl came in and started into Mr. Quinn's office. Noticing Ella who was writing the message for Mr. Quinn on the note pad, she came closer to introduce herself. Ella assumed she was Billie.

"You must be Ella Raines. Mr. Quinn told us you were coming in to work today. I'm Billie Long."

"Hello. I just took a telephone message for Mr. Quinn."

"Would you like for me to put it on his desk? I was just going in."

"Oh, yes. Thank you. It was nice meeting you."

"It was nice meeting you, too. See you."

Billie was a slim girl of medium height with light brown hair and brown eyes. Her manner was friendly and her smile welcoming. She went into Mr. Quinn's office and sat at her desk across from her boss's. For a few minute all was quiet. Ella finished glancing through the last of the files and put them back on Frankie's desk.

Mr. Quinn returned a few minutes later. When Frankie returned from lunch shortly afterwards, Ella caught a whiff of onions as she approached, sat down, and reached to store her purse in the bottom drawer of her desk.

"Were there any calls?"

"Just one for Mr. Quinn."

Frankie put a stick of gum in her mouth and dropped the paper in the trashcan nearby before answering.

"Mr. Quinn's wife hasn't been well lately. She has trouble with her nerves, and every time she gains weight she has a setback."

"Oh, that's too bad."

"Yes. She's been in the hospital I don't know how many times."

"My mother suffers from a type of mental illness called paranoid schizophrenia," Ella replied. "It causes her to feel that everyone's against her. She's been in the hospital several times, too."

Just then Cecil came into the room to consult with Frankie about a shipment to be made.

Frankie smiled at him while she cracked her gum, and her eyes glanced over him while he asked her about the shipment. She picked up one of the files on her desk, quickly thumbed through the contents to the page she was seeking, and answered his question.

"Stone wants a thousand yards this week, and another thousand yards next week."

"Both shipments to be finished goods?"

"Yeah. They're making children's pajamas from it."

Frankie engaged him in a little chitchat, her eyes reflecting the smile on her lips. Ella noted that her eyes spoke eloquently of her moods. Before, while Frankie had been explaining some of Ella's duties to her, Ella had noted that her expression had been flat and her descriptions careless and rather vague. Now, however, her eyes gleamed with interest as she and Cecil continued their conversation. Cecil looked at the sheet of paper in his hand and turned to go.

"See you later, Frankie."

"Okay. Bye."

Ella totaled some of the invoices on the calculator, and typed them after Frankie had checked her figures.

Later, Mr. Quinn called her in to take dictation. They were short, fairly simple letters. After she'd finished typing, she took them in for signing. He'd left his door open after lunch. Billie looked up and smiled politely as if her mind was still on her work. She was involved with a thick bank statement. The afternoon passed quickly until it was time to punch out and go home.

The next few days went by uneventfully, and soon she'd worked her first week. She wouldn't get paid until the following week, however, as her first week's pay would be held back.

Monday morning rolled around again, and the days passed faster as she was gradually given more responsibility.

Billie frequently stopped by Frankie's desk to chat. Her hair was rather thin, but its wispy tendrils suited her rather gamin face. Her top front teeth protruded slightly, but they, too, suited her face and added to her attractiveness. She and Frankie included Ella in their conversations, which made Ella feel more at home. When she ran out of something to do, she would roll her chair over to lean her elbows on Frankie's desk.

Today Billie's face lit up as she laughed at some of Frankie's remarks. She had a quick mind, and returned Frankie's friendly teasing with some witty quips of her own, her expression mischievous and her brown eyes sparkling.

Ella soon learned that Frankie enjoyed gossip and that she tried to extract juicy tidbits of information from others at every given opportunity.

Ella had begun to relax, and as she became accustomed to the new machine, her typing improved.

It was with surprise that she was called into Mr. Quinn's office one morning to find Frankie sitting by his desk. Mr. Quinn had some files there, one of which was open in front of him.

"Frankie tells me that you haven't been ordering the greige goods on schedule for Stone Manufacturing Company."

Ella had learned that greige goods were unfinished material. She felt her face burn with shock and bewilderment and she gave Frankie a look that expressed her feeling of betrayal. Ella was at a loss. She thought she'd been fulfilling all her responsibilities. Confused, she could think of no defense and remained silent as Mr. Quinn gave her the brunt of his displeasure. He pointed to a yellow carbon copy in the file.

"These orders have not been made, and from now on they will be made on schedule. Do you understand me?" His voice rose in anger.

"Yes, sir."

Ella gave Frankie another hard look and caught the undeniable look of self-satisfaction on Frankie's face, as if she was pleased with the situation and thrilled at Mr. Quinn's censure.

"Frankie, I want you to show Ella how the orders are to be made and explain the schedules to her so that this will not happen again in the future. It must not!"

He looked at Ella again and his last words issued a final warning.

"Yes, sir."

Ella felt belittled and angry with Frankie for having gone to Mr. Quinn instead of personally showing her the errors. Noting Frankie's smug expression, her eyes stung with tears as she followed her out of Mr. Quinn's office. Frankie had the open file that Mr. Quinn had used as one example of Ella's shortcomings. She pointed to some dates and yardages on the copy of the letter that held the ordering schedule. As Frankie explained it to her, Ella saw at once what had not been done.

This must be what I missed that first day when I failed to listen carefully to Frankie's instructions. I was looking at her instead of listening to what she was attempting to explain to me. I didn't realize then how important it was. That sure won't happen again!

"Look through the other files and make sure that all the greige goods have been ordered on time."

It was impossible for Ella to speak so she nodded, picked up the stack of files, and carried them to her desk. While Frankie was explaining how the shipments were to be ordered, her pride had forced her to school her expression to hide her hurt feelings. She didn't want to give Frankie the further gratification of seeing her so close to tears from the altercation for which she was responsible. Ella was grateful that she could now turn her back to Frankie.

Settling down to work, she worked her way through the files with focused concentration, deaf and blind to anything else. She was determined not to make any more errors on the shipments. When she heard the phone ring and Frankie's greeting as she answered, she refused to let it register.

When Billie came out of Mr. Quinn's office to ask Frankie a question, she didn't look at them and listen to their conversation. She would have the day before. She worked on until it was time for the others to take their lunch breaks. After finishing her work, she checked over each file carefully to make sure she'd made every order as scheduled. Failing to find any overlooked shipment orders, she leaned her chin on her hand and looked out the window, reflecting on the morning's events.

She accepted the fault as her own, but resented the way the matter had been handled.

Maybe it's good that it had happened as it did. I must be more responsible. Instead of spending so much time listening and looking at what's going on around me and talking to Frankie, I have to concentrate on my work. I just can't lose this job. Doris would be so mean and sarcastic if I did. I don't think I could stand it.

But her trust had been damaged. She realized that Frankie would stab her in the back again if she got the chance. Since Frankie thrived on gossip, she would repeat any remark that she might hear Ella innocently make about her co-workers. From now on, her ears would be open but her mouth would be closed.

She had met Faye Brown from the warehouse, and had learned that she worked with Cecil and Otis, the husky black man who appeared to have the strength of two men. She'd met him on her way to the restroom at the back of the warehouse, and had seen him lifting heavy boxes ready for shipment. He handled bulky rolls of cloth as if they weighed but a few ounces.

Faye always spoke to her in passing and she seemed friendly. She was kind when Ella had a question about an order. Cecil was nice as well, when she had the rare chance to visit the packing warehouse.

The warehouse was cold in winter, but cool in summer because it was unfinished inside. The studs and rafters were exposed, and the tall loft rising to the roof plus two large ceiling fans kept the warehouse cool in the summertime.

Faye came into the office from the warehouse frequently to file packing slips.

She stopped by Ella's desk occasionally to chat, or sometime Ella joined her while she was filing and they'd talk for a few minutes.

Ella estimated Faye to be in her early to mid-forties. There were a few gray hairs running through her dark hair, and a few lines were beginning to form at the corners of her eyes. Rather than detracting from her attractiveness they added to it. Her sweet disposition reflected the beauty that was within. Her brown eyes and dark complexion went well with her dark hair. A sharp mind was evident in her quick movements and efficiency in her work. Sometimes Ella overheard her asking Cecil how to best fill an order or perhaps how to pack a particular shipment.

She may not be the more experienced of the two, but she has a lot of common sense.

She'd also noticed that Faye's eyes lingered on Cecil's an instant too long, and there were a few other little things that made her uncomfortable.

Oh, it's just your imagination working overtime. Don't get so carried away.

It was Frankie that told Ella that Faye and Cecil had a thing going. Frankie didn't seem to feel the least compunction as she spilled the details of their relationship; both were married. On the contrary, Frankie seemed smugly satisfied, as if she took pride in their affair. She wasn't above flirting with Cecil herself.

Cecil was husky, with blue eyes and brown curly hair, and he seemed a bit shy the few times she'd been in his presence. Her instinct told her, however, that even though he didn't talk a lot, he was thoughtful by nature, thinking things through before finally reaching a sound decision. Perhaps that was what attracted Faye to him. She knew she could depend on him.

Everything settled into a comfortable routine until that fateful Monday morning when the entire office was thrown into turmoil. Ella had clocked in as usual, but she felt something in the air that told her all wasn't right. Everyone looked more serious than normal, and there wasn't the bantering and chitchat that usually started the new week.

The sober looks she met as she passed her co-workers on the way to her desk puzzled her. Then she remembered seeing the big boss's car in the parking yard as she'd started up the front steps. Something was brewing, but she didn't know what. Both of Mr. Quinn's doors were closed, and she knew he was inside with Mr. Eugene Stone, III. It was unusually early for Mr. Stone, since he normally visited either just before lunch or shortly after.

Billie came out just as Ella reached down to store her bag in the bottom drawer of her desk. Billie's eyes looked a little red and she held a tissue to her nose. She rushed toward the restroom. Ella heard her sniffing as she left the room.

Ella's thoughts went back over the past few weeks. Hers was not a vindictive nature, and she forgave easily. She and Frankie were on better terms, and she had become better acquainted with Billie. She and Mr. Quinn were getting along and she conscientiously did her work.

One reason she got along better with the girls was that she needed them. Since finishing school, she'd lost touch with most of her classmates. Many had gone on to college or to jobs here and there.

Her mind drifted back to her high school days. She'd worked in the lunchroom all three years of high school in order to receive free lunches. Her family had been on a limited budget and it was the one way she could help out. Her job in the lunchroom was to wait on the teachers' tables. They sat in a separate group from the students, and had more flexibility in their choices on the menu. She'd take each teacher's order, give it to the ladies in the serving line to fill, and then carry the lunch tray to the teacher.

Sometimes she'd give the wrong order to a teacher or get a choice wrong, but the teachers took it good-naturedly and so did she. Walking to school had saved bus fare. She was glad that she'd been able to work for her expenses. Otherwise she would have felt a burden to her financially hard-pressed family.

Working in the lunchroom left her little time to be with her few friends, but at times it worked out so they could eat lunch together.

She came back to the present as the door to Mr. Quinn's office opened.

Mr. Stone came out followed by Mr. Quinn. They were both serious and subdued. After walking together to the front, they paused for a short period of discussion. Mr. Quinn came back alone and closed himself into his office.

Billie and Faye came back into the office together. Billie seemed to be feeling better. Faye looked sober, but had no visible sign of tears.

Frankie looked from one to the other as they neared her desk and asked, "What's wrong? What's happened?"

Billie's eyes filled with tears, but she controlled her emotions and replied, "Mr. Quinn's been accused of embezzling money from the company."

Ella thought of Mr. Quinn's wife's many illnesses and hospitalizations. Even if he had insurance, of which she was not sure, doctor and hospital bills could mount up quickly. She had a feeling that he'd felt his back was to the wall and he'd siphoned it off in desperation.

"What's Mr. Stone going to do?" Frankie asked, a morbid interest in her eyes.

"I don't know yet. The auditors will have to go over the books to find out exactly how much is missing."

Faye had remained silent, but now she spoke.

"Will they let Mr. Quinn go? Will we lose our jobs? My husband has a bad heart condition and I have to work."

Billie looked at Faye and replied kindly, "Since Mr. Quinn has been with the company for so many years I don't think they'll press charges. He and Mr. Stone have been good friends for a long time. They'll probably just retire him."

Mr. Quinn didn't come out of his office all day, nor did he call Ella in for any letters. The girls went on with their regular work, but they had a lot going on in their thoughts. Disbelief, shock, sympathy, and uncertainty were emotions they all shared.

The next day the auditors came to check the books and Billie was shut in with them most of the day. Mr. Quinn didn't come into work that day. He said his wife wasn't feeling well.

Frankie and Ella went on with their routine tasks and for once, Frankie didn't chatter as much as usual. Ella was rather glad for she, too, had a lot to think about. She shared Faye's anxiety about her job. She enjoyed her job and didn't want to have to look for a new one.

She asked Frankie, "Did Mr. Quinn have any children?"

"He has one son but he's lived somewhere out west for years. They aren't very close. He barely knows his grandchildren."

Ella felt grateful for her Y.W.A. group. One or two were former classmates at school and went to her church. Aside from her friends at work, the girls were her only social contact and she gained spiritual inspiration from their meetings. Their leader, Mrs. Benston, was a warm caring person, and she occasionally invited them over for supper and a sleepover. Tonight was their meeting night and she looked forward to seeing Mrs. Benston and the girls. She hoped to get a chance to tell them about the situation at work and perhaps have a special prayer with them, all of which would help ease her anxiety.

Mr. Quinn never returned to his job at Economy Textiles. Billie, who apparently had contact with him once he left, told the girls that he had retired and he and his wife were moving to Florida.

He did the best thing under the circumstances. It would have been awkward for him to come in to tell us goodbye.

Billie told them that they would be getting two new managers who were being transferred from Stone Manufacturing Co., the parent company for Economy Textiles.

They would be sharing Mr. Quinn's old office. To Ella's surprise, Frankie Styles was being transferred to Stone Manufacturing Company with a promotion and new job.

Billie would be using Frankie's old desk, Mr. Mitchell took Mr. Quinn's old desk, and Mr. Cheney took Billie's. In time, a receptionist was hired, Nita Davis, and also a new bookkeeper, Sarah Wills.

With so many changes taking place, it seemed like a different company to Ella. She began taking on new responsibilities like computing the invoices, with Mr. Mitchell checking them before she typed them. He checked them again before they were mailed.

The first day she took dictation from Mr. Cheney, he gave her a long letter, which she just managed to hold to one page. She had taken it in for him to sign and had returned to her desk when she heard him exclaim loudly, "Boy, have I got me a secretary!"

Panic filled Ella as she heard his statement. She'd merely done her job, just as she'd done with Mr. Quinn.

Why does he have to act like that? I wish he'd just kept his big mouth shut!

She felt frightened and self-conscious, and all her newly acquired security seemed to have disappeared. The unwanted attention made her feel uneasy and insecure. She was not accustomed to it and didn't know how to handle it.

Criticism and disapproval were the emotions that she'd lived with at home. In fact, since her father had died when she was ten years old, it was all she could remember. Sometimes it seemed that nothing she'd done had been right. If she did something right, it was not acknowledged nor had she received any credit for her good behavior. Her mother and older sister, Doris, were constantly fussing at her about something, which lowered her self-esteem and self-confidence so that she had no faith in herself. In her emotional and mental immaturity it never occurred to her that her mother and her sister were under a great deal of emotional and mental adjustments, as well—her mother without prior preparation in dealing with the responsibility of earning a living; her sister being a year behind in school, struggling to keep up with her subjects as a consequence; trying to make the money stretch while grocery shopping and planning meals from one month until the next, and dealing with two growing girls as they neared their teen years.

Having a twin sister made it difficult to develop her own personality and sense of identity. They'd dressed alike until high school when it finally became impossible to find clothes alike in the same size. Everyone seemed to expect that because they were identical twins, they must be exactly alike. They shared their classes, activities, and experiences. Since finishing high school and working at different jobs they weren't together as much, and were learning to depend less on one another.

Bringing her thoughts back from the past, she rolled her chair around so that Mr. Cheney would see only her profile. She'd have to figure out how to handle him and come up with some kind of game plan.

Suddenly she remembered Aunt Grace, her mother's sister who was two years older. She was the one who'd encouraged Doris and the younger girls to take business courses in high school so they'd be prepared to support themselves. Aunt Grace had been a secretary, also, in the days when it was considered "forward" for a woman to work as a secretary. She also remembered Aunt Grace's warning about men they'd be working for, and to be on their guard for inappropriate attentions from their boss. Aunt Grace had shared an experience she'd endured on her first job, when her boss chased her around his desk. She'd left and gone to work for a man who had his office in the basement of his home. He had a wife and three children. After she'd worked for him for several years, his wife developed cancer of the "female organs." She'd died with it after suffering lingering pain and gradually growing weakness for a year. Her boss had eventually asked Aunt Grace to marry him, and she became wife, secretary, and mother to his children. Ella's family, that is, her other aunts and her cousins, had thought that Aunt Grace had "set her cap" for him, because he had his own business and did quite well, and she became a member of the upper class in society, going to bridge clubs, gardening clubs, and entertaining social events in her home. Uncle Mac's friends and business acquaintances had accepted her, but it took a long time for his family to accept her. " Did Aunt Grace's warnings about men influence her discomfort around Mr. Cheney?" she asked herself.

She opened one of the files on her desk and began looking through it for greige goods shipments to be ordered. She'd learned that greige goods were unfinished cloth that had to be finished, that is, dyed to order and sized. Sizing meant giving the material a glazed finish so that it was ready to be fashioned into garments.

When it came to the day-to-day operation, Mr. Mitchell and Mr. Cheney often deferred to Billie's years of experience with Economy Textiles. Mr. Cheney would ask her to get the party he wished to speak with on the phone, and then take over the call. She took some letters, too, and was an administrative assistant to both men.

Ella admired Billie very much, and approved of everything about her even down to her handwriting. As she'd done with Frankie, she'd roll her chair over to Billie's desk and prop her elbows on it when she ran out of things to do. She and Billie had taken the Gregg system of shorthand and could read much of each other's dictation. Billie would help Ella when she'd get stumped on a word she couldn't read back. Much of the time, Ella would suddenly realize what it was before Billie could translate it.

"Oh, now I remember what it is!" she'd say, and roll back to her own desk to finish typing the letter.

Mr. Mitchell also dictated letters to her, and he had an embarrassing habit. He appeared to be nervous when giving dictation and would anxiously rub his hands between his thighs as he talked. Ella was shocked the first time she'd witnessed it, and she and the other girls discussed it among themselves.

"It's just a nervous habit. I don't think he's even aware that he does it," Nita said during one of their conversations. "It's sort of like biting your fingernails or twisting your hair."

Ella tried to force herself to ignore it. She finally learned to glue her eyes on her shorthand pad and refuse to look at him. When he'd pause to search his mind for a word that eluded him, she'd stare at her shorthand pad and wait for him to continue. Fortunately he didn't dictate long letters to her as Mr. Cheney did, and he didn't use her skills often.

Sitting at her desk one day, her thoughts drifted back to her home life and the fact that her family had never really communicated with each other. Her mother and sisters avoided the subject of sex at home; the mid-Victorian standards toward sexual matters were still in place. As a consequence, she felt that sex was vulgar and distasteful. She was over-sensitive when the subject was mentioned, and she was uncomfortable in even the mildest sexual situations. In fact, she'd even been unprepared when she experienced her first monthly period. Other girls in her class had begun their periods much earlier. But then, she'd always been small and immature for her age and was past thirteen when she had her first period. It hadn't really concerned her because she figured that eventually she'd get around to it at the right time. Oh, she'd known about menstruation, thanks to Doris. That was one good thing she'd done for the girls. She'd just felt surprised and unprepared when it happened, emotionally unready. Doris gave her the things she'd needed and she'd felt better about it.

Her thoughts drifted back even further in the past to when she was nine years old. She remembered when her mother was having such heavy periods, that she'd overheard her telling Doris that she was "flooding," and seeing bloody cloths soaking in a pail of water. She'd stay in bed during the worst days of her heavy flow. It was also at this time that the doctor began treating her mother with hormone shots. He called it "going through the change of life." She'd begun feeling severely depressed, and both her father and the family doctor were optimistic that given enough time her moods and behavior would improve. It soon became apparent after a year's time, however, that the shots were not bringing about the hoped-for change, but rather that her mental health was deteriorating rather than improving. It was then that her father told her and her twin sister not to show that they were afraid of her. He was tender hearted and hated to put her in the state hospital, where mental patients were admitted. It was terribly over-crowded, an old hospital made up of several buildings, with the men separated from the women. Some patients had to spend the rest of their lives there because at that time they didn't consider that there was a cure for mental illness. He'd felt he could deal with it by her staying at home.

That was the reason he'd talked to them, and tried to prepare them for what lay in the future, as her behavior became less connected with reality. They were frightened of her at times, such as when she'd hack on the back door frame with a butcher knife—or make odd remarks to the girls in a manner that was not normal for her. As her behavior became increasingly erratic, and these frightening episodes occurred the girls would run outside and stay for hours. The doctor assured them, when her depression began and it became apparent that she was emotionally distraught, that she would harm herself rather than someone else. Toward the end she was unable to take care of the house or the girls, and Doris was forced to miss eighth grade to care for the household chores and look after her younger sisters. It was then that Doris assumed the parental role that she eventually was cast in permanently.

One day, while Ella and her twin sister were playing outside in the yard, they heard something that they assumed was a car backfiring. The next instant, Doris called out to them from the back door.

"Both of you come quick. Mama just shot Daddy. I think he's dead!"

Ella and her twin sister ran toward the house. Ella went into her parents' bedroom where her father had been sleeping. He'd worked the third shift at the Union Bleachery Mill and slept in the afternoons. Her mother had become paranoid, and was jealous of the woman who rode with him to work. They'd worked in the same department, the dyeing room, and on the same shift. Of course, there was no cause for her jealousy—it was all in her imagination.

Perhaps Doris is mistaken. Maybe he isn't really dead.

Ella leaned over him, touching his shoulder and noting the position in which he'd been lying. A pool of blood was on the pillow behind his head. He'd been shot in the back of the head. Her mother had gotten his shotgun and loaded it before shooting him. He'd always kept the shotgun, unloaded, in the corner of the hall leading to the back porch.

"Daddy," she said softly, but she knew he couldn't hear her. She accepted the fact that he was dead, but she lingered just a moment longer. It was her way of saying goodbye. Glancing around the room, she saw the blood spatters everywhere...on the dresser, the walls, and the curtains.

She heard Doris talking to her mother in the dining room, just off the hallway, with the bedroom where Ella still stood over her father, also off the hall opposite the dining room.

"Mama, why did you do it?" Doris said accusingly but sadly, too. She knew that her mother didn't know what she was doing, and probably would never remember it, but couldn't help but feel anger and grief. She knew that it would be a blessing if her mother remained unaware of her crime, and it seemed to be the case. Later, when she was well enough to come home from the state mental hospital the subject of how he died was never again referred to.

Her aunt, her mother's sister, came at once when she got word. Ella and her twin sister were taken to Aunt Grace's house, and from then on it was never mentioned. No one seemed to want to talk about it, but Ella wanted to talk about it. She wanted them to say what they were feeling so that she could express her own feelings. But at that time there was a stigma attached to mental illness. Families who were affected by it tried to keep it hidden and didn't discuss it.

At her father's funeral, the family went for a final look at him in his casket. Ella overheard one family member say, "He looks so peaceful…like he's asleep."

It was comforting to Ella to hear that because it sounded so normal; like he'd somehow wake up and everything would be okay. But she knew that he'd gone to Heaven to be with his Heavenly Father. In spite of her sadness, she felt reassured because she knew that one day she'd see him again. After the funeral the girls went to live with Aunt Ella, another of her mother's sisters. She was forced to make the adjustment of living in a new home without either of her parents and at the same time going to a new school. Aunt Ella lived across from the high school, and Ella and her sister walked the three or four blocks to the elementary school, Anderson Street School.

They'd made some friends who lived nearby and usually walked to and from school with them. One day, one she would never forget, they'd happened to be walking home with one particular girl who had a tendency to gossip. She'd asked Ella and her sister, "Didn't your mother kill your father?" Ella had felt as if the ground had dropped from beneath her feet. She'd never felt such sickening fright in her life. It was a shock she'd been unprepared for, because it was never discussed at home, and she never dreamed that in moving from the country into town someone would find out about it. Her twin sister had the presence of mind to come up with an answer. "No, he died of pneumonia." She had borrowed from the past because her father had suffered pneumonia twice. For Ella to hear her father's death spoken of in such cheap gossip made her feel ill; her heart beat with such heavy thuds she could scarcely breathe. She had been so close to her father and had loved him with all her being, and in addition to feeling his loss now she had been found out with some terrible secret. It'd felt like her whole world had stopped and she had nothing else to live for. She'd felt the most unreasoning fright that she was helpless—she couldn't even think.

Gradually, however, she felt more secure as it wasn't mentioned again. The girls remained at Aunt Ella's until school was out that year. They'd finished the fifth grade and were promoted to the sixth grade. For that summer all the girls, even her oldest sister who had finished school and worked in a bank, went to stay with her brother and his wife and baby. The "twins" as they were often called were allowed to take their niece outside in her baby carriage and roll her around the block. This thrilled them immensely because they would meet people on the sidewalk who would look at the six-month old baby, and pride swelled in their hearts that they were allowed this responsibility. One afternoon Louise, the baby's mother, was unable to get the baby to sleep for her afternoon nap. Ella took Judy, her niece, and laid her on her knees and began rocking her in the rocking chair. Singing some hymns to her as she rocked, she was eventually able to get her to sleep, and was proud that she was able to accomplish this helpful task.

Her mother had been in the hospital a year, and when she was able to come home she and the girls went back to Aunt Ella's and lived in an apartment on the opposite side of her big house, until they could get settled. At first Ella felt shy and unsure of herself with her mother when she first came home from the hospital, but it soon changed to a natural and close relationship between them. They were able to finally get a duplex apartment in a government housing project, and Ella and her family lived there until Ella finished high school. These were the happiest days of her life, growing up in the housing project with a family that was close to each other. Of course, they had their ups and downs and the girls had to be corrected as in all families, but for those years she would take nothing. The girls had friends their age to play with, and during the summer they'd play outside until dark playing "kick the can". They could see even after darkness fell because the streets were well-lighted; there were outside lights in front and backyards, and at the end of each block. For the first time she could remember she had emotional security and the happiness of growing up in a close neighborhood and feeling accepted.

She snapped to the present suddenly and looked around her. No one seemed to notice that she'd been daydreaming. Did Mr. Cheney remind her of her father?

He has the same dark hair, and his eyes are gray or hazel...but daddy's eyes were blue.

She picked up the pieces and went on with her work. It had been a long time since she'd remembered it all, but it felt good to realize that she'd once had a father and mother, and there were still some childhood memories in her mind.

Ella began to go through a distressing period. She would get nervous giggles over the most casual statements and would often start laughing at the most inopportune times. She'd try to hold them back when someone was talking, either to her or to someone else in her presence, but sometimes she just couldn't stifle her laughter. It was so embarrassing and she didn't know what to do about it. She talked with her older sister, Doris, about her problem.

"Men like girls who laugh and are vivacious."

"But I get them at the worst times! It's like being hysterical or something. I can't seem to control them."

"It's probably just a phase you're going through. For goodness sakes, don't worry me about it. I have enough to worry about already!"

It took a while, but she finally did get over it. She realized that she simply hadn't known how to handle awkward situations. Her self-consciousness made her feel that everyone was looking at her, and she didn't have the poise and self-assurance needed to deal with such situations calmly.

She met a boy and had begun dating. Her time with him boosted her self-confidence and helped her to relax when in the company of the opposite sex. She'd met Bobby Callaham at a church social her Y.W.A. group had planned. Several of the girls had brought a date.

Ella hadn't known anyone to invite so she'd gone with friends. Later he'd asked her out to a movie.

Ella surmised he'd gotten her phone number from the girl who'd invited him to the party. Soon they fell into a routine of going to a movie, sometimes a drive-in, and eating hamburgers and sodas at Cahaly's, a popular hangout for the local teenage crowd. He never attempted to get mushy and didn't even try to hold her hand. They found themselves forming a friendship of habit, and it made her feel as if she were like everyone else her age - like she belonged. Unknown to her, another problem loomed on the horizon. She soon found out that she was more ill at ease around men than she had thought.

It happened one Monday morning when Mr. Cheney called her in for dictation. Nylon tricot was a hot item on the textile market. Mr. Cheney had begun dealing quite a bit in this new material, and was selling it to buyers for manufacturing ladies' underwear. He'd been dictating a long letter, when suddenly he began describing the style of a particular women's undergarment: a new type of women's panties with a cotton-lined crotch. At home she was used to seeing her bras, slips, or panties drying on the wooden clothes rack everyone used for underwear. With no men around she never gave it a thought. But when Ella heard this frank description, she was so shocked and embarrassed that she was unable to think. She bowed her head and raised her hand to her forehead, forgetting everything but her shame and humiliation at being subjected to such a vivid description of women's intimate apparel.

"Are you all right, Ella?" Mr. Cheney asked.

She was unable to look at him, much less answer him. She tried desperately to pull herself together.

"Yes, I'm all right."

He continued his dictation and she automatically wrote down his words. She wasn't conscious of what she was writing, and she didn't even consider if she would be able to read it back. She was like a wooden automaton whose pencil moved over the pages of her shorthand pad, writing symbols by rote, as if she had become wound up to function until she ran down. At last he was done and, still in a state of shock, she walked back to her desk and sat down.

She sat for a moment and then stood up, walked over to the cola machine and, using the coins she kept in her desk drawer, put them in the slot and pushed the button. Opening the bottle, she took a swallow and felt it burn all the way down her throat. She took another drink, feeling the sting of the carbonated water reach her stomach, and finally felt the hot flush leave her face. She stared out the window as she finished drinking her soda and then slowly walked back to her desk.

She sat down in her chair and began typing the letter. She felt exposed, as if she had nothing to hide behind. Shock still held her in its grip and she didn't know what to do about it. If only she could tell someone about it. Perhaps Billie would understand. After all, they were from a similar background. She decided to confide in her.

Holding her shorthand pad out to Billie she asked, "Would you read the first paragraph at the top of the page?"

"All right."

When Billie finished she looked sympathetically at Ella.

"Oh, honey, I can just imagine how embarrassed you were. But it had nothing to do with you. To him it's business—what Stone Manufacturing Company does. He didn't think about how you'd feel because it meant nothing to him. Just forget it. Put it behind you and go on as if nothing happened. We feel this way because we are women. Men can't understand these things. Just accept that and know that we understand one another. That's enough."

Billie returned Ella's shorthand pad, squeezed her hand, smiled encouragingly, and both returned to their work.

The Christmas season was rapidly approaching and the girls began planning the company party. They discussed it with the men and decided to hold it at the Poinsett Hotel. The hotel had several private dining rooms and the food was excellent. Ella thought about what she would wear. She remembered buying a piece of tiny red and white checked taffeta. She decided to have it made into a suitable dress and, of course, she'd invite Bobby to accompany her.

That afternoon she took the material, pattern, thread, and zipper to Mrs. Mason, the dressmaker who sewed for her now and then. The pattern had short puffed sleeves and a square neckline cut a bit lower than she normally wore. Mrs. Mason grasped the tape measure in her hand and held the pattern pieces up to Ella's back and then to her front. Then she began taking Ella's measurements.

"You're no bigger than a minute," she said as she measured Ella's waist. "With this full skirt you'll need to wear a crinoline petticoat under it for the dress to look right," she mumbled through several straight pins she held in her mouth.

She needed to adjust the pattern to make it small enough for Ella. Although Ella had long legs and arms, she was short through the waist, which made her difficult to fit.

The next day she went shopping on her lunch hour for shoes and an evening bag to match her new dress. The only shoes she could find to fit her narrow feet were silver evening sandals, and she purchased them as well as a matching beaded silver bag. Satisfied that she had her attire well in hand, she worked steadily through the rest of the day, listening to the other girls' discussion of the event and what they would wear.

"I'm sure they'll serve champagne," Nita said. "I heard Mr. Mitchell ordering the menu. He ordered shrimp cocktail, steak, baked potatoes, and salad. Doesn't that sound delicious?" Her green eyes were filled with excitement. "Of course, for those who don't drink they'll have ginger ale," she added.

That'll be me. I wonder what Bobby will drink.

Several days later she went for a fitting at the dressmaker's shop. When she tried on the dress, even with straight pins still holding it together in places, she couldn't help but get excited. She looked at her reflection in the full-length mirror. The material shimmered and the style was becoming to her slim figure. The full sleeves and square neck flattered her small waist, and the crinoline petticoat billowed out below to accentuate her slim curves.

"Oh, Mrs. Mason! You've outdone yourself this time, for sure!"

Mrs. Mason had used all her skill to make the dress a perfect fit.

"For an important event like the office Christmas party, it had to be right," Mrs. Mason said with a wink.

Mrs. Mason helped her out of the dress and Ella slipped back into her work clothes.

"You can pick it up tomorrow. I'll have it ready for you."

"You will? Gosh, that'll be great!"

At last the big night arrived. Ella had washed and set her hair the night before and it shone with golden highlights. The dress drew attention to her brown eyes, fair complexion, and light brown hair. She'd decided to wear a narrow red velvet ribbon around her hair, tied with a bow in front. The ribbon brought out the red checks in her dress.

She heard the peal of the doorbell and knew it must be Bobby. She hurried to the door in sandals that had higher heels than she was accustomed to wearing.

"I hope I don't fall flat on my face," she thought, as she opened the door to Bobby. He looked very handsome in his black suit, white shirt, and black bow tie.

He smiled at her." Gosh, you look swell. Are you ready?"

"Yes, just let me get my bag and stole. I may need it later."

Bobby's waistline was slightly chubby, but since he was tall, he carried his bulk well. They arrived at the hotel and saw that everyone was there in their best bib and tucker.

"I believe we're just about all here so let's take our seats," Mr. Mitchell announced.

Bobby and Ella found their seats and Bobby politely pulled out Ella's chair. She smiled her thanks and looked across the table to see who was opposite them. There sat Mr. Cheney and his wife.

Great. Just great.

She stared as if hypnotized as his eyes measured Bobby, and then moved on to her. Ella felt he was curious about their relationship, and for a reason she couldn't explain, she suddenly felt shy and tongue-tied. She fiddled with her silverware and took a sip of water from the sweating goblet.

She was glad when the waiters began to bring their food trays around and serve each guest. She looked at her shrimp cocktail and hoped she knew which fork to use. Her steak was a little too rare.

I'll just eat around the outside edges. They're not as red as the center.

After everyone had begun eating their meal, Ella attempted to converse with Bobby. Evidently, he also felt a little out of place. He answered her in monosyllables, and she noticed that his usually sallow complexion looked a little red.

The headwaiter began to serve the champagne. He opened the bottle and deftly caught the foam with his white cloth. Ella put her hand over her wine glass when he came to her and he politely poured her ginger ale instead. She noticed that Bobby had accepted a glass of champagne and looked at him questioningly.

"I've never tasted it before," he explained in a low, nervous voice.

"Oh, I haven't, either. I just didn't want to make a fool of myself. Anyway, I don't drink."

She watched him take a big gulp of his champagne. He began coughing, covering his mouth with his napkin.

She caught Mr. Cheney's eyes on them as if he was still curious about their relationship and was analyzing them. When he met her glance, his eyes narrowed speculatively. Her heart beating rapidly, she met his stare and then turned her eyes away. She felt like everyone was staring at them. She tried to eat her meal but it tasted like sawdust.

Ella and Bobby didn't linger long after the supper was over. She was introduced to Billie's husband, El, and Nita's husband, Dave, and they chatted for a few minutes. Everyone else seemed to be enjoying the champagne, but since it was getting late, she and Bobby decided to say goodbye. She walked over to Mr. Mitchell and his date, and Mr. Cheney and his wife, who were standing together.

Looking at each couple she said politely, "We had a nice time. Have you met Bobby Callaham?"

Mr. Mitchell and Mr. Cheney shook hands with Bobby.

Mr. Mitchell said, "Nice to meet you, Bobby. How did you manage to steal Ella away from all the other boys?"

Bobby blushed. "Just lucky, I guess."

Mr. Mitchell then introduced them to his date, Christine Martin, who was a tall, pretty brunette. Mr. Cheney, in turn, introduced them to his wife, Lorraine. She was a redhead with the usual freckles, but her brown eyes made her quite attractive.

"Well, I guess we'll say goodnight since tomorrow is a work day." Ella included them all in her farewell glance.

Thank goodness tomorrow's Friday!

"Goodnight, Ella. Glad you made it." Mr. Mitchell shook both their hands.

"Goodnight, Ella, Bobby." Mr. Cheney nodded to both of them.

The next morning started off pretty much as usual. Faye came in to the office to work with some cloth samples. She sat at a desk that was next to the file cabinets across the room. Ella walked over to chat with her for a few minutes.

"We missed you last night, Faye."

"I would have come, but my husband didn't feel well. I hated to leave him when he was having chest pains. He has angina and takes nitroglycerin tablets which helps with the pain most of the time, but it's still scary to leave him alone when he's experiencing it."

"I'm sorry he wasn't feeling well."

Just then Mr. Cheney came out of his office and approached them.

"Faye, please see if you can find this packing slip for me. I've looked for the number but can't find it."

After looking at the number of the packing slip, Faye got up from up her desk to pull out one of the file drawers. She, too, failed to find it.

"I really don't have the time to keep up with them, Mr. Cheney. Sometimes I get behind because of my other work. Here are some I haven't had time to file. I'll look through them and see if it's there."

But the elusive packing slip still came up missing.

"Since Faye doesn't have time to keep up with the filing, Ella, I want you to go through every drawer and folder in this cabinet and make sure they're all filed right. Get Faye to show you how she does it," he instructed the girls.

Faye explained to Ella that the slips were filed in numerical order, some with four digits and some with five or six. Those of a series were filed in the same folder. The tab was labeled with the series of numbers the folder contained.

Ella had a natural affinity for the task and enjoyed the challenge. She always carefully looked at the number on the packing slip before she filed it to be sure she put it in the right folder.

A few days later Mr. Cheney approached her.

"Ella, see if you find this packing slip for me. I'm on the phone and need it right away." He handed her the bill of lading. She looked at the number and quickly located the correct folder. She searched through it, found the right one, and then handed it to him. He took it and hurried back to his desk and the waiting customer on the other line, but not before she saw the look of satisfaction on his face.

After he left her, Ella realized she took pride in locating a packing slip quickly. She was gaining much-needed self-confidence in her successes. It was not to be taken for granted, however, for she knew there was always the possibility that she could make a mistake and file one in the wrong folder.

Ella was beginning to realize, at last, that the reason she felt so nervous and tense around Mr. Cheney was that she was afraid of him. He made her feel vulnerable. Since her father died when she was barely ten years old, she'd had little close contact with men. To her they seemed like beings from another planet.

Now that she was better acquainted with him she realized that at first she had not trusted him. Her shyness had kept her on edge, and she'd felt tense and unsure of herself. But in time she learned to be more comfortable around him. Now she was learning to feel a deep respect and admiration for him. Her feelings had changed without her being aware of it.

She realized also that she no longer felt so uncomfortable around Mr. Mitchell when she took letters from him. In one way, she felt a kind of pity for him. She was aware that his behavior was odd, but she understood that he couldn't help it.

All of us have our little idiosyncrasies, I guess.

She reflected back to the first day she'd come to work at Economy Textiles. She had changed since then. Her self-confidence had grown and her personality had matured.

She recognized that the girls she worked with were responsible for much of the growth and she thought with a grateful humor, "I owe you one." For the first time since she'd been in the high school band, she felt she was an equal part of an organization.

She also felt gratitude to Mr. Mitchell and Mr. Cheney, for they, too, had contributed a tremendous amount to her growth as a person. To work with and get to know them was a chance that she appreciated. She knew it was an experience she'd never forget.

THE INCIDENT

The metal front door of Economy Textiles felt hot to her hand as she closed it to leave for lunch. This was her first job upon graduating from high school, still two months short of her eighteenth birthday. Economy Textiles was only one of many textile companies in her hometown, most of them cotton mills. Unfortunately, it was located in a rather seedy part of town. A few blocks away were a beer parlor, a run-down hotel with an unsavory reputation, and a greasy spoon restaurant.

As she started the four-block walk to Main Street and its main shopping area, the heat hit her in the face like a fiery fist. For the past couple of days, temperatures had soared to the one hundred degree mark, unusual for a town located so near the mountains.

Ella walked the short distance down the driveway and onto a short, unpaved road that led onto River Street, and further down, the River Street Bridge. The Reedy River flowed under the bridge and was polluted by nearby industries that dumped their wastes into its waters, causing an unpleasant smell.

She continued over the bridge to the intersection of River Street and the cross street that curved around on each side. River Street continued straight under a railway trestle. There was no signal here, so upon descending the few steps from the bridge to street level, she had to be alert and fleet of foot to make it through the four-way traffic safely. She crossed it without mishap and began trudging up the hill toward town. The glare burned her face and eyes, and she decided to purchase a pair of sunglasses while she was out.

There were three ten-cent stores, a hot dog and orange juice eatery, several large department stores, four movie theatres, two jewelry stores, a couple of furniture stores, and two nice hotels in the six block shopping section of Main Street. The three ten-cent stores had luncheonettes, so there were ample choices of eating-places.

Ella had climbed halfway up the hill. She planned to turn right onto Main Street once she reached the top. But before she got there, a car pulled up beside her and stopped. A man's face leaned out the open window on her side and spoke to her.

"How's Doris doing these days?"

Since Ella's older sister's name was Doris, she assumed he was either a former co-worker or an acquaintance of her sister.

"Just fine," she replied, not wishing to be rude.

"Is she still working at the G &N Railroad?" His eyes moved lazily over her hair and eyes before lowering to her mouth, chin, and throat.

"Yes."

She was beginning to feel uncomfortable as his gaze traveled idly downward to the sheer yoke insert of her printed voile dress and lingered there momentarily. Her face flushed and his gaze returned to her face once more.

He asked casually, "Would you like a ride?"

At first she thought he was politely offering her a ride uptown to avoid the heat, but as she looked into his face, she realized that wasn't his intention at all. Obviously he thought she was one of the streetwalkers who frequented the area close to her place of work, or at least a girl who knew her way around and was familiar with this part of town. He was trying to pick her up! Her face flushed in anger and embarrassment and she said in disgust, "Oh, I thought you were someone else."

Turning away from him, she continued to walk toward town, upset by the incident.

Puzzling over in her mind as to his identity and how he seemed to know her sister, Doris, she was unable to come up with a logical conclusion. He wasn't a co-worker of her sister or he wouldn't have asked such questions about her.

When she returned from lunch, she told the other secretaries about the incident.

"He was probably just trying to pick you up. You know what this part of town is like. He may have thought you would be taken in by his attention because you're so young. Young girls are often strung along then left once the man gets what he wants," Billie advised. "I'm glad that you had more sense than to get into his car. There's no telling what might have happened."

"He was certainly up to no good, that's for sure. Why, he might have carried you out to a deserted area and killed you!" Nita's green eyes grew big as she let her imagination have full rein.

"Okay, girls. Let's not get carried away," Ella said. "I'll ask Doris about him tonight. Perhaps she can clear up the whole thing."

"Yes, that's the best thing to do. Keep calm, and don't go off half-cocked until you have more information," Sarah agreed.

The girls settled down and returned to work and Ella tucked the incident to the back of her mind until she could talk with Doris about it later.

That evening at the supper table, she told Doris about the incident and asked her if she had any idea who the man might be.

"No, I haven't the faintest idea. I'll think about it some more, though, and ask the men at work about it. They may have seen some drifter hanging around the rail cars."

"Thanks. I'd appreciate it."

A few days passed, and Ella mentioned the incident again to Doris.

"Have you come up with anything on the man who tried to pick me up the other day?"

"No. I checked with my boss, and all the freight workers and the engineer, and they agreed they haven't seen any strangers around the car yards."

"Oh, well. I'll probably never run into him again. Thanks for the detective work, though." Ella said with a smile.

The next day Ella decided she wanted a sandwich and cherry cola from Carpenter's Drug Store. It was a combination drugstore and lunch counter. Its soda fountain and homemade sandwiches made it a popular place to eat.

There were several booths that seated four, so they had adequate serving space without holding up the lunch crowd with a long wait. Arriving at the drugstore, she chose an empty seat by the window through which she could observe the passing traffic while she waited for her order. She idly watched the cars pass and stop at the red light on Main Street.

Suddenly her attention was riveted to a navy blue sedan that crept by behind two other cars as they approached the red light. The driver was the man who'd tried to pick her up last week. She was sure of it!

She quickly turned toward the soda fountain so her back was toward the window. She hoped he hadn't seen her. For some reason she felt frightened.

What threat could he possibly be to me?

Just then her order arrived and she tried to concentrate on eating her lunch, but her mind raced.

So what if he did see me. It's a free country. I can go anywhere I want.

When she returned from lunch, she told the other girls that she'd seen his car pass the drug store.

"Oh, that doesn't mean anything, Ella. He probably works somewhere near here and was on his lunch hour, too," reasoned Billie.

"Yeah, I guess you're right. No use borrowing trouble."

"I usually have enough without borrowing more," remarked Sarah Wills, the bookkeeper.

Ella and the other girls laughed at Sarah's whimsical statement and then settled down to work.

The day had been hot and humid so Doris and Ella settled on a chef's salad for supper. They enjoyed the cool meal, and afterward each carried on their individual pursuits. Suddenly the telephone rang. Ella was closest to it so she took the call.

"I saw you at the drugstore today. Did you enjoy your lunch?"

Ella recognized the voice on the line immediately. Slamming down the receiver, she stood trembling, staring at the telephone as if it were a rattlesnake.

Doris looked up. "Who was that?"

"It was the man who tried to pick me up the other day. I'm sure it was his voice."

"Really? He doesn't seem to take no for an answer."

"Well, I think I'm going to report him to the police tomorrow. I don't like him hanging around me."

"Certainly can't hurt. There's no harm done if he doesn't contact you again."

The next day Ella walked to the police station, which was a couple of blocks down on the other end of Main Street. To her disappointment, no one seemed to know how to help her. One officer suggested she try the Magistrate's office, which was upstairs in the courthouse.

She trudged several more blocks to the courthouse and gladly rode the elevator to the second floor where the Magistrate's office was located.

The Magistrate was out, but his secretary informed her that the Magistrate no longer handled matters of this kind. They were now the responsibility of the Sheriff's Department.

"Where is the Sheriff's Department located?" Ella asked.

"It's four blocks away, about two blocks down from the Police Department."

"I was just there and they sent me to you!"

"I'm sorry, but as of the first of the year we no longer deal with cases of harassment and matters of that nature. The laws have changed, and these cases are now under the supervision of the Sheriff's Department."

"Thanks." She tried to hide her frustration.

Ella was now determined that someone was going to help her, even if she had to go to the Attorney General himself. She headed off to the Sheriff's office, but when she looked at her wrist she noticed that she was using up a big part of her lunch hour.

Well, I'll just grab a sandwich and cola and eat it at my desk.

She finally reached the Sheriff's office and asked the receptionist if she could see the Sheriff.

"I'm sorry. He's out to lunch. But the Deputy Sheriff should be back in about fifteen or twenty minutes. Would you care to wait?"

"Yes, I'll wait. Thank you."

Her determination was building by the minute.

How does anybody know where to go with a law enforcement matter, and then how do they get anyone to help them once they find the right place?

The minutes ticked by, but at last her wasted lunch hour began to seem profitable. The Deputy Sheriff walked through the front door and pulled off his sunglasses, tucking them into his shirt pocket.

"Deputy Ross, this young lady would like to see you," the receptionist told him, motioning toward Ella who was sitting on the edge of her seat.

The deputy sheriff smiled at her, and walked over to shake her hand. "I'm Deputy Sheriff Ross. Let's go into my office where we can talk privately," he offered, gesturing for her to go ahead of him. "It's the second door on the left."

"Thank you."

Ella walked ahead of him, a flicker of hope lighting in her that, at long last, she would get some help and information for her problem. He went to his desk and offered her a nearby chair. When they were comfortably seated, he asked, "Now, how may I help you?"

"A man stopped me on the street a few days ago and began asking me about my older sister, Doris Raines. He seemed to know her because he knew where she worked. Then he started getting fresh. He asked me if I needed a ride and he stared insultingly at me when he talked. I knew then that he was trying to pick me up. What I don't understand is how he knew my sister's name and where she works."

"You talked to your sister about the incident?"

"Yes, but she has no idea who he is. She even questioned her boss and the other men who work for the railroad."

"Do you think you'd recognize him again? Do you know what kind of vehicle he drives?"

"I know I'd recognize him again. While I was eating lunch yesterday, I saw him drive past Carpenter's Drug Store. He had to slow up behind a couple of other cars that were approaching the red light. I didn't think he noticed me, but he did. After supper, he called me at my home. He told me he saw me there and asked if I'd had a good lunch."

"And the vehicle he was in—was it a late model, or an older model? Could you identify it?"

"It was an older car, a dark blue sedan, but I don't know what model or make. Since I neither have a car nor drive, I'm not familiar with the many makes and models."

"I see. But you can give me a description of the man?"

"Yes. I think he was of average height, though I've only seen him in his car. I'd guess him to be probably around 5'9" or 5'10" with a medium build and dark hair. He wore dark glasses so I don't know the color of his eyes. His complexion was average, and his nose was crooked, like he may have broken it at some time."

"Any scars, moles, or other identifying marks?

"Yes, he had a scar on his right cheek, maybe an inch or an inch and a half long that went into his hairline."

"You're a very observant young lady," the sheriff commended her.

"He approached me so that his right profile was at the open window. He kept tapping nervously on the steering wheel while he talked to me."

"Like he was jittery and unaccustomed to picking up young ladies?"

"Yes, I believe so. He seemed to put on a front of sophistication, but it didn't exactly ring true. He looked me over in a suggestive way, as if he knew his way around, which made me both embarrassed and mad. But I'm not sure he is the type who does this sort of thing all the time."

"When he called, did he try to get you to make a date with him?

"No. I slammed down the receiver when I recognized his voice."

"So you knew his voice when he called you?"

"Yes, sir."

"He hasn't sent you any gifts—flowers, candy?"

"No, sir."

"Has he threatened you or any member of your family?"

"No, sir."

"And you say he tried to pick you up, you saw him through the window of the drugstore, and he's called you once, making a total of three contacts?"

"Yes, sir. That's right."

"Hmm...he hasn't followed the usual behavioral pattern of a stalker. My gut feeling is that something triggered his odd behavior, causing him to act completely out of character. Since we have no identity, no exact description of the vehicle, and no information on his domicile or place of work, the only thing we can do right now is sit tight and wait to see if he makes further contact. If he does, I'll need to know immediately. Any further information you may come up with will be helpful."

He reached into a small, compact container on his desk and handed her one of his business cards.

"Call me if you see or hear from him."

"Thank you very much, Deputy Ross. I was beginning to think that no one would help me. If he does anything else and gets caught, what will happen to him?"

"Well, the Code of Laws for the State of South Carolina was changed at the beginning of this year. Right now everyone is still a little confused and uncertain where they stand right now, but they'll catch on before long.

As to what will happen to him, if he turns himself in there will be no sentence. He'll be referred to the local Department of Mental Health for counseling."

"Thank you again. You've made me feel much better."

Ella reached out to gratefully shake his hand again for his help and understanding.

"Call me if you need me."

"I will. Thank you for being so reassuring."

"No problem. That's what I'm here for."

Ella had used up her lunch hour by the time she arrived back at work. She settled for a pack of crackers and a soda from the snack machine, and sat at her desk to eat her meager lunch.

Mr. Cheney, her boss, came out of his office and looked at her light lunch with a question in his eyes.

"You must have had a lot of shopping to do today."

"No, sir. I was at the Sheriff's office and didn't get a chance to have lunch."

Needing someone to talk with, and sensing his genuine interest, she told him about the incident and the unusual stranger.

"Have you seen or heard from him since?"

"Yes, sir. I saw him at lunch yesterday from the window in Carpenter's Drugstore.

Apparently he also saw me, and he called me last night to ask if I'd had a good lunch."

"So you went to the Sheriff's Department to talk to someone about it?

"Yes, sir—the Deputy Sheriff. It took almost my entire lunch hour to find someone who could help me. First I went to the Police Department. They sent me to the Magistrate's Office. Once there I was told to go to the Sheriff's office as the state laws had changed as of the first of the year and those matters are now handled by them."

"So you recognized him and his car?"

"Yes, sir. I don't think I could ever forget either one. His car was a dark blue sedan, but I don't know the make or model."

"Well, the important thing is that you'd know it if you saw it again and that you could recognize him."

"Yes, sir. His nose was crooked, as if it had been broken, and he had a scar on his right cheek near his hairline. He had dark hair, but I couldn't see his eyes through his sunglasses."

"Well, be careful, and let me know if you run into him again."

"I will. And thank you, Mr. Cheney."

Ella carried on her day-to-day activities for a couple of weeks with no more confrontation with her unknown mystery man. He seemed to have vanished completely.

Deputy Ross called to see if she'd seen or heard from him.

"I checked through the wanted files, those who have a record as a stalker or harasser of women, but I didn't find anything to match his description, or at least what information we have on him thus far. Either he doesn't have a record or he's never been caught. My instinct tells me that he's emotionally disturbed, but not to the point of being dangerous or of harm to anyone."

"That sounds good, I guess. I mean, I don't have to be on edge or as fearful as I would if he had a record of this sort of thing."

"Probably not. Just continue to be careful and let me know at once if he contacts you again. It's a good sign that he's remained silent thus far. He still hasn't sent you any flowers or gifts of any kind, has he?"

"No, nothing. That would be a bad sign, wouldn't it?"

"Yes. It would show that he had developed an obsession with you, as most of these types of criminals do when they develop a love obsession or fixation on a person with whom they have no personal relationship. I'll check with you again in a few days."

"All right, Deputy Ross. Thank you."

A few more days passed, and still Ella hadn't seen or heard from the strange man. Her job kept her busy. Since it was now spring, business was heavier than ever. Shipments were being ordered for fall clothing. Manufacturers had to keep a season ahead to have a new line ready when the season changed.

A few days after her call from Sheriff Ross, she was surprised to be summoned outside by both Mr. Mitchell and Mr. Cheney. Wondering what was the matter, she opened the front door and hesitantly walked out onto the stoop before descending the steps. Her eyes opened wide as she saw the dark blue sedan parked in the yard. Mr. Mitchell and Mr. Cheney stood on either side of the car, preventing the occupant from leaving.

Ella walked toward the group, her eyes full of questions as she neared the vehicle. Mr. Cheney opened the door on the driver's side and allowed the young man to get out. He stood by the car and looked at Mr. Cheney with a silent plea in his eyes.

"Ella, I believe this young man has something he wants to say."

"Yes, I certainly do. First of all, Miss Raines, I want to apologize for my recent behavior and I'll try to explain it. You see it all began when my girlfriend broke up with me and told me she never wanted to see me again. I guess I kind of went crazy because I was hoping we could eventually get married. So when I saw you on the street that day, it struck me that you closely resembled her. I suppose I tried to associate the two of you together, believing that I could get back at her through you.

Last night she called me and asked if we could get back together. She invited me over and we had a long talk. As we talked, and as I thought about what I had done, I realized that I have some serious emotional problems. I think I need some counseling.

Today I turned myself in to Deputy Sheriff Ross. He didn't sentence me. He only referred me to the local mental health center for proper counseling. I've already set up my first series of appointments. Best of all, Joan and I are going to be married as soon as I get my head straightened out.

I came here to apologize for bothering you like I did. I promise it will never happen again. Will you forgive me?"

"Yes, I forgive you. By the way, what is your name? I don't know what to call you."

"Oh, I'm sorry. I'm Timothy Johnson. And the men told me you are Ella Raines."

"Yes, these are my bosses, Mr. Mitchell and Mr. Cheney." Ella indicated which of the men was which.

"Nice to meet you both. I can see how well you look out for Ella, if I may call her that, and how lucky she is to have such good bosses."

"There's one thing I'm curious about, Timothy. How did you know my sister's name was Doris?"

"Oh, I work for UPS and make deliveries to the G & N a lot. I mentioned to one of the men at the freight yard how much you and she favored one another, and he told me that the two of you are sisters."

"Well, for heavens sake! I would never have guessed that. I'm glad you and Joan are back together, and I wish you well with your counseling sessions. I hope that you will both be very happy once you're married."

"Thank you very much. We want to pick out an engagement ring tomorrow on our lunch hours. I just got off work and I wanted to see you, if possible, before you left for the day. Again, I want to say how sorry I am for worrying and probably frightening you. I just was out of my head there for a while."

"Well, they say that all's well that ends well, and I feel this is the end of this incident." Mr. Mitchell shook the hand that Timothy extended to him, as did Mr. Cheney.

"God bless you both. I'm glad that Ella works for such a good company. I appreciate your being so nice to me. And Ella, I will always be grateful to you for forgiving me. It wasn't an easy thing to do but I'm glad that you did."

"Best of luck, Timothy."

"Thank you, Mr. Cheney."

"I wish you well, too, Timothy. Hope things work out for you in the future."

"Thanks, Mr. Mitchell. I hope so, too. Well, I'll go now. Joan has asked me over for supper tonight and I don't want to be late. She's a real good cook and I know she's going to make me a wonderful wife. She'd have to love me for sticking by me like she's doing. I certainly love her."

Echoes of goodbyes followed Timothy as he entered his car and drove off, waving a hand in farewell as he made the turn out of the yard of Economy Textiles.

For a moment, all was quiet, and then the three of them started back into the building.

Mr. Mitchell spoke as they entered the front office.

" I believe this calls for a celebration. Everyone, go get your favorite soft drink. The drinks are on me." He grinned at his own pun and they all laughed.

"Yes. I agree that all's well that ends well. I say we close up a little earlier than usual. That's my contribution to everyone," suggested Mr. Cheney.

Ella's eyes glistened with tears of relief as she took the soda that Mr. Mitchell handed her. All the other girls had joined them, as they had witnessed all that had happened. They were all abuzz with happy comments as they each chose a soft drink from Mr. Mitchell's selections.

It was with a lighter heart that Ella left for home that afternoon. She said a silent prayer of thanks to God for working things out for her. Her favorite scripture verse came to mind as she began her walk to the bus stop. She whispered it to herself as her eyes misted with grateful tears.

"And we know that all things work together for good to them that love God, to them who are the called according to His purpose." Romans 8:28.

Her heart was full as she reached home and entered the front door to call out to her sister, "Guess what, Doris! The incident is closed!"

FAREWELLS MUST COME

Ella Raines had begun working at Economy Textiles only a few months out of high school. Now that she was becoming better acquainted with the other girls, she felt more comfortable at her job.

Nita was the receptionist at the front desk. Although she was older, she and Ella had become good friends. The other girls were of varying ages.

Nita had not used her typing skills after finishing school. After marrying, she had remained a homemaker until her children entered school. She was nervous about her typing, which had become rusty from disuse. Ella tried to help Nita whenever she could.

"Ella, would you help me with this letter? I've got to have it ready for Mr. Mitchell. Please tell me if it looks all right or if you think I should type it over."

Ella felt as if their roles were reversed and she was the older of the two. She read the letter carefully. It had several erasures that were not skillfully done. Plainly, it was not typed neatly enough to give to Mr. Mitchell to sign.

"Just re-type it, but take your time. Don't get excited. Just concentrate on one word at a time. As you get better at it you'll make fewer mistakes. Then you'll begin to build up your speed. Believe it or not, my typing teacher told me she didn't think I'd ever learn to type and I took it for two years! So don't give up. You can do it."

"Okay, but I want you to look at it after I re-type it, okay?"

"Sure. Just let me know when you're ready."

Nita's second letter looked better. She had fewer erasures and they were less noticeable.

"That's much better. See what I mean? You're already on the road to better days."

"Thanks, Ella. You're a life saver."

"Anytime, Nita. Just remember that old saying: 'Practice makes perfect.' Only after I came to work here did I build up my typing speed and accuracy."

Nita made an effort to follow Ella's advice and soon her letters began to look neater. If there were more than the three erasures allowed by her typing teacher, they were neatly done. Ella's affection for Nita grew as they worked together. Nita did not know shorthand, so she took dictation in longhand. Over the next couple of weeks, as Ella continued to check over Nita's letters, she felt like a teacher who sees her pupil reach his or her potential. Ella's encouragement had a visible effect on Nita's confidence, and her typing improved until soon she no longer needed help.

Ella learned to appreciate the girls' friendship and whenever the men were away, the girls would gather together in a group. Nita would stand guard if they happened to get together at Billie's desk, two offices down the corridor. The girls would stop their conversation and wait for Nita to see if the coast was clear. It was inevitable, however, that they would have some close calls. Each girl would then scurry back to her desk, trying to stifle the laughter that threatened to erupt before the men entered their offices.

Sarah, a tall, attractive girl with an olive complexion and dark hair and eyes, was the next girl to come on board after Ella. She wore her hair short with a side bang that she was constantly pushing to the side out of her eyes. Her figure was well shaped and a little buxom. Although aware of her charms, she was not conceited. The dimples in each of her cheeks became more prominent when she smiled, which she did often.

Sarah paid the bills, balanced the bank statements, made the deposits, and did monthly reports on money spent and taken in.

Billie, whose desk was next to Ella's, was the administrative assistant to both of the bosses. She had light brown hair, dark brown eyes, and had a ready sense of humor. She was from the lower part of the state and had an attractive low-country drawl. When she made a witty remark or quip, her sparkling eyes gleamed as she heard the appreciative laughter from her audience.

Ella took dictation and typed invoices for shipments. Many of these were made to companies in New York City, in the heart of the garment industry. Ella's company was a buyer for Stone Manufacturing Company, one of the large sewing plants that made children's underwear and play clothes.

Faye was in her early to mid-forties and was the oldest of the girls. She had dark brown eyes and black hair that was beginning to show a few gray hairs. She worked in the warehouse with Cecil and Otis packing up orders for shipment. Ella sometimes had to go to their department with a question regarding a shipment, for which she had to compute the invoice.

She'd noticed little things between Faye and Cecil that caused her to suspect they were romantically involved. They both were married. When she learned that they did have a thing going, she was disillusioned and wasn't sure how to act around them. It made her question her own beliefs regarding faithfulness, morality, and her judgment of others.

She also became self-conscious around Mr. Cheney, from whom she frequently took letters. She reasoned that if Faye and Cecil, who she formerly believed to be trustworthy, could carry on an affair, someone else like Mr. Cheney might do the same thing. Although she had previously been relaxed in his presence, she began to doubt herself and tried to concentrate solely on her work whenever he was around. It didn't always work.

She began to notice what a nice-looking man he was. It frightened her when she had those thoughts, and she hoped that her face didn't betray her admiration. She was also fearful that he might begin to think of her in a new way, which made her uncomfortable whenever she had to go into his office.

There were times when she was taking dictation that he would pause to collect his thoughts, or take a moment to make a long-distance call before he completed dictating a letter. She'd sit quietly, waiting for him to finish his call or proceed with the letter. These occasions were uncomfortable for her. She squirmed when she found his gaze upon her as he talked or laughed heartily with the other party, laughing again before he finally hung up the phone.

Ella's father had died when she was barely ten years old. After that she had little contact with men and because of that lack of contact, she was shy around them. She didn't have the self-confidence needed to deal with them in a work-a-day world.

While Mr. Cheney dictated a letter she tried to concentrate fully on her shorthand, writing out a word in longhand now and then when he paused for a moment, to be sure she'd be able to transcribe it correctly later.

The more uncomfortable she became, the more she looked to her faith in God to help her make sense of her feelings and thoughts. She'd say a prayer for His help before entering Mr. Cheney's office. It helped strengthen her weak faith, which had not been truly tested prior to the present situation. Still, she struggled on shaky legs. Daily she turned to the God she had trusted since childhood. He gave her an inner peace and a new humility. She looked to Him for guidance. Finding one's own philosophy is a natural part of growing up and is a process that all young people have to undergo, whether their philosophy becomes good or bad. So she sought her Bible and read God's promise to never leave nor forsake her. Because she'd placed her trust in Jesus Christ as her personal Savior she had the promise of eternal life both here and in Heaven with Him. This belief gave her courage. There were the good times, however, and Mr. Cheney seemed unaware of her struggles, as did everyone else. She did not know that her co-workers saw the change in her personality and that her faith was a positive influence upon them.

There was a new sweetness about her, and they noted that she never used profanity or told ugly jokes. When they occasionally told an ugly joke she never laughed because she usually didn't get the point. She had a new depth of character and serenity that they wished for. They realized she was different because she was a Christian. She inspired them and they respected her because she lived what she believed.

In time they all grew close as if they were one big family. She had a new freedom to be herself. Mr. Mitchell addressed all the girls, or women as the case would be, as Miss Nita, Miss Billie, etc., an old Southern custom that showed respect.

The girls shared one another's problems and gave help whenever possible. For instance, Ella suffered cramps with her menstrual period each month. Billie advised her, "Don't wait until your stomach begins to hurt badly. As soon as you start your period, take one of these tablets. The stomach cramps are what make you feel nauseated. Also, drink a cola or some kind of soft drink with it. The caffeine will make the pills take effect sooner."

She tried the tablets and they helped the cramps, but they caused drowsiness and a rapid heart beat. One day when all was quiet, she crossed her arms over her typewriter and laid her head down for a few minutes. Upon hearing footsteps approaching from the warehouse she sat up, but not before Mr. Mitchell entered the office area. He gave her a sharp look as he passed by going to his office. Her thoughts went to the times she and the other girls had discussed Mr. Mitchell's odd behavior while dictating letters; he'd nervously rub his hands between his thighs.

"I don't think he even realizes that he does it. It's just an unconscious habit, like biting your fingernails or twisting your hair," Nita would tell them.

Ella was embarrassed when she first had to take dictation from him, but discussing his behavior with the other girls had helped her to accept it. She simply she kept her eyes focused on her shorthand pad.

Her emotions were affected from the way she'd been brought up. Not being around men in her family and seeing their weaknesses and strengths, yes, and even idiosyncrasies, did not prepare her for the real world. In her home sex was touched upon rarely as if it were a subject that was shameful; she was affected more by what was not said than what was actually mentioned. Having no men around to see her underwear drying upon the wooden rack used for small things didn't prepare her to hear her panties, bras, and slips mentioned, because with an all female household they were taken for granted.

Nita had told the girls some details about her family. Nita's married name was Davis, and her husband's first name was Dave. Ella thought this was an unusual combination. Nita was very family oriented and had a sweet and understanding nature. One day, in one of their conclaves while the men were out, the subject of pregnancy and birth came up. Ella remarked that she thought people could choose whether or not to have children. Then she could have bitten her tongue because Billie and her husband were unable to have children.

"You mean you don't believe that God causes us to conceive and children are His gifts to us?" Nita asked, shock and amazement reflected in her expression.

Ella carefully thought over Nita's question. Nita's sincerity of faith radiated from her whole personality.

"I suppose I never thought of it like that."

Ella continued as though thinking aloud, "In my home the facts of life were not discussed. My mother was the youngest of eight children and was born when her own mother was forty-two years old. My mother's older brothers and sisters were born in the early to late 1880's. My mother was taught that sex was vulgar, and not to be discussed. Consequently, she taught my sisters and me by example, mostly, the principles and teachings with which she herself had been raised. My mother was born in 1901 when the influence of the mid-Victorian period was still strong so she knew no other way to behave, or for her to teach us to behave and think. Sex was just something a woman had to put up with, and we were taught that menstruation and having children were the curse that God put on Eve for sinning in the Garden of Eden, and consequently upon women since then. Women were not supposed to enjoy sex, but to give in to their husbands' sexual needs; that was what their husbands expected."

The older girls nodded and smiled in agreement with Ella, signifying that they, too, had been taught similar morals.

"People today don't think that way, Ella. It's the 1950's and things have changed. But I suppose it still affects people's emotions who were brought up that way," Nita told her.

Nita is a lucky person, and with her warmth and wholesome outlook on life, her family is blessed to have her for wife and mother.

Billie responded, "I know. Our emotions affect us in all kinds of ways."

" Let's change the subject to something more pleasant. For instance, I'm lucky to have my husband's mother with me. She usually has supper ready when I get home, unless either she has plans to go out, or El and I decide to eat out. Sometimes El and I go to the Dairy Queen for lunch. I love their cheeseburgers, fries, and milkshakes. But I can't eat there too often or I'll get too fat." She wrinkled up her nose playfully, for she was thin, almost skinny.

"You don't have to worry about being fat yet, Billie," Ella thought.

Ella asked Sarah, "Aren't you from Virginia?"

"Yeah, I grew up in Roanoke. We lived in Lynchburg for a while, too. My Dad's company moved him around. That's how I ended up finishing high school here."

"Wasn't that kind of rough on your family, having to change schools so often?" Billie asked.

"Yeah, sometimes. But my Mom never worked outside the home. She was always there when we came home from school, so that helped. But now I think she's having a hard time going through the change of life. She says whenever she's out somewhere and experiences a hot flash she just has to get out right then, no matter where she is. She's had to leave her buggy full of groceries in the store because she had one."

"Oh, how terrible," Ella said.

The other girls nodded in sympathy with the problem suffered by Sarah's mother.

The next day, Faye was working with some cloth samples at one of the desks on the opposite side of the room from Ella. When Ella got up to take some letters for Mr. Cheney to sign, she heard Faye call her name softly and looked up. Faye motioned for her to come over to her desk.

"You've got a spot on the back of your dress."

"Is it bad?"

"Pretty bad. Come on. We'll go to the restroom and I'll wash it out and iron it dry. Just leave your letters here, and you can take them to Mr. Cheney when we get back."

"Oh, would you? I would really appreciate it."

Faye kept an iron and ironing board in the restroom to use on wrinkled cloth samples. Once there, she lifted up the back of Ella's full-skirted dress. Wetting the spot in the lavatory with a small amount of cold water, she applied soap and rubbed gently. In a few minutes, the spot came out; after rinsing it she set up the ironing board and plugged in the iron. In a few minutes the hot iron had done its work and the dress was dry and clean as ever.

"I really appreciate your doing this, Faye. I didn't know the spot was there. Maybe I can return the favor some time."

"I'm glad to do it. We girls have to stick together." She winked at Ella who smiled.

As a result of Faye's kindness, Ella and Faye's relationship became a close one. Ella soon forgot about Faye and Cecil's affair and accepted her as a friend. Faye began to stop by Ella's desk, or Ella would walk over while Faye was filing packing slips, and they'd chat for a few minutes each day.

Ella had begun bringing her lunch, and Faye teased her about getting a little tummy from eating so many sandwiches.

One day she confided to Ella, "My husband has a very bad heart. The girls and I go to the hospital to see him every night. When I sit on the edge of his bed, I feel his heart beating so hard it shakes the bed." Her anxious face revealed her concern about his condition.

"Well, I hope the doctors can help him and he can come home soon."

"I do, too. It's wearing me out."

Soon another opportunity came for the girls to bunch together. The men had to meet with the executives of the parent company, Stone Manufacturing Company, which was some distance away. That time away left the girls alone to talk.

Sarah was the first one to begin the conversation. Her boyfriend, Tommy Jones, was the subject.

"Oh, I know Tommy Jones. He was in one of my classes in school," Ella said.

"Yeah, I'm a year older than he is. Anyway, his father walked out on them several years ago and his mother just went to pieces. She's staying with his older brother, so Tommy went to live with his older sister and her husband. He finds it hard to believe that anyone loves him. I tell him that a lot of people love him, including me." She held out her left hand and smiled, her dimples playing hide and seek on her cheeks. A diamond solitaire engagement ring sparkled on her ring finger.

"He gave it to me last night," she said, holding up her hand for the others to see.

All the girls admired the ring and congratulated her on her engagement. Sarah dipped her head and showed her dimples in that slightly sheepish smile she had, pleased with the attention she was receiving.

"After you're married, though, I believe he'll feel more secure," Billie assured her.

"Marriage has matured me, and it will Tommy, given enough time."

Sarah looked at Billie with hope in her eyes. "You really think so?"

"Yes, I do. It will help both of you. You'll draw closer to each other, in a different way than you are now. Romantic love is wonderful, and a honeymoon lets you enjoy it, but you have to come back down to earth sooner or later to really get to know one another. They say you never really know anyone until you've lived with them. Then you'll have a deeper appreciation for one another."

"Say, didn't you go out with Mr. Mitchell a couple of months ago?"

"Yeah. I dated him a couple of times before Tommy and I became serious.

The first time wasn't too bad. We went out to a nice place to eat and afterward, he tried to get mushy, but I said it was getting late so he took me home. The second time, after we had eaten, he parked the car in front of my house and before I could stop him, he had his hands all over me. I had trouble pulling them off. Who would have thought a man his age would act like that?" she asked of the group. "I mean I went through the parking and petting stage in high school!"

"Well, a man's always a man," Billie remarked sagely. "I dated this guy once and he tried to get me to go to a motel with him on our first date! I'm so glad I met El and we got married. He's so sweet. I have to tell you, though, on our honeymoon, when I woke up the next morning and saw a black-haired man next to me with his head on the pillow beside mine, it gave me a funny feeling."

"How's El doing these days? His real name is Elzie, isn't it?" asked Faye.

"Yes, but everyone calls him El. He's not doing too well. The doctor says he has an enlarged heart, which causes him to cough. It's really rough when he gets a chest cold. The only thing he can prescribe is plenty of rest. But the way El loves working on trucks, it's going to be hard to get him to relax and take some time off."

Billie's husband and his brother had a good business servicing commercial trucks, often working late into the night to get a job finished on time.

"El's good at keeping the books, isn't he? Maybe he could start doing most of the business end and get a part-time mechanic to help with the truck repairs," Nita suggested.

"That's a really good idea. I'll suggest that to El. He may just go for it."

The girls drew closer together as they shared their problems with each other, often drawing from their own experiences to offer helpful solutions.

The company didn't have many people passing through, and even Mr. Richardson of Stone Manufacturing Company only dropped by every two or three weeks.

Ella remembered the day he told her that her slip was showing. She was embarrassed so she ignored his comment. He picked up on her discomfort but didn't understand her behavior. He told several others gathered in Mr. Cheney's office, "I told Ella her slip was showing, and she acted like it made her mad."

Frustrating as it was, she could only react according to her upbringing.

Billie took him aside and told him quietly, "Didn't anyone ever tell you that you shouldn't inform a young lady that her slip is showing? Here in the deep South it just isn't done."

Mr. Richardson, from one of the northern states, had the grace to blush faintly and nod his head in understanding.

"Thanks for informing me. I'm always running into these southern traditions. Heck, I'm from Michigan. How am I supposed to know?"

"Well, next time just whisper to one of the other girls to tell Ella that her slip is showing. It probably embarrassed her, and she didn't know how to react. She's been brought up in a family with no men around and she didn't know what to say."

To compound the problem, Ella wasn't feeling well that morning, anyway. As her period had started she was moody, and Mr. Richardson's saying her slip was showing was the last straw. Not knowing what to say, she said nothing.

Perhaps a hot drink would help her to relax.

She walked over to the coffee maker that was kept full of hot water for coffee, tea, or cocoa. A cup of hot cocoa suited her taste, and while she spooned the right amount into her cup, poured in hot water, and stirred it well she thought of her mother.

That was another thing which didn't help her feelings--she was worried about her mother, who had suffered several nervous breakdowns during Ella's eighteen years. Glancing at the calendar that hung on the wall, she realized that next week would be her nineteenth birthday. Where had the time gone? As her thoughts returned to her mother again, Ella feared that it wouldn't be long until her mother would have to return to the mental hospital, her only recourse of treatment.

Her fears were justified the next morning as her older sister, Doris, told her that the sheriff's department was going to take her mother to the hospital by ambulance.

"They'll be here at 8:30 this morning. She won't be up so I doubt if she'll have time to take any of her things with her. I think it's better this way. She won't have as much time to get upset."

Both sympathy and relief filled Ella; sympathy that her mother had to suffer so, and relief that she would be getting the care and treatment that she needed. She would be going to the state mental hospital, which was always overcrowded and understaffed. Ella hoped they would be able to help her mother to recover from her deep depression.

Those shock treatments can't be good for her, but what other choice do we have?

After she had arrived at work this morning she had punched her time card just barely on the dot of eight. Her workday was from eight until five o'clock. She'd headed for her desk, hanging her jacket on the coat rack on her way, and stored her bag in the bottom drawer. It was hard for her to concentrate on her work, because she knew what was happening back at home, but she tried to focus on the stack of invoices on the table beside the calculator waiting to be computed. She worked until she finished them, and then glanced at her watch. The hands pointed to nine-thirty.

Mom's already gone...

She was suddenly overcome with grief, remembering that Doris had said her mother would not be able to carry anything with her. Helpless to hold back the tears, she began walking quickly toward the warehouse and the restroom at the back. She grabbed up a few tissues to wipe away the tears that began trickling down her face. Thankfully, she reached the restroom and sat down in a chair, giving vent to the deep sobs that racked her body. In a few minutes she heard the door open and Faye came in. Ella looked up, still crying openly.

Faye stood beside her and patted her on the back. Ella told Faye what happened as best she could through the sobs that refused to stop.

"Go ahead and cry, honey. It will help you to get it all out."

Ella continued to sob, but gradually she grew quieter and was able to talk. She'd confided to the girls that her mother was mentally ill and needed help, so they were aware of the situation. She'd not told Mr. Mitchell or Mr. Cheney, but felt sure that one of the girls would have already talked with them about her mother's illness. Feeling a little better, she went to the lavatory and splashed cool water on her face, hoping to remove some of the traces of tears and the redness from her eyes.

"Here, honey. Here's a washcloth and towel," Faye offered, holding them out to her.

"Thanks."

Ella wet the washcloth and held the cool fabric against her eyes. It felt good against her hot cheeks.

"She'll be better off, Ella. Maybe they'll help her to get well."

"I know. I just wish she could have taken her own things with her. She'll have to wear those awful hospital gowns, and dresses that don't fit, and whatever shoes and underwear they can find for her. It'll be two weeks before they'll let us visit her."

"Well, you can look forward to going to see her. You could take her some of her favorite food and other things you think she'd like. You know how hospital food is." Faye screwed up her face to express her opinion of hospital food.

Ella tried to smile. Blowing her nose, she told Faye, "I guess I'd better get back to work."

"You stay here as long as you need to. The work will wait."

While she was getting her emotions under control, Ella thought seriously of her relationship with Faye. Faye's depth of character had been brought about through her husband's illness. Ella felt Faye's experience had caused her to have more compassion and a desire to help others. Perhaps her own experience of sharing her mother's suffering from recurring bouts of depression would help her to gain the same depth of character and compassion that Faye possessed.

She'd come to look upon Faye as almost a mother substitute. She had a deep admiration for her, despite the rumors of Faye's affair with Cecil. Perhaps that was her way of dealing with her own problems.

"You know, Faye, my father died when I was barely ten years old. With my mother in the hospital so much, many times I had neither father nor mother at home. Only Doris was there, trying to play both roles. With no men around, I grew up feeling they were beings from another planet. I was terribly shy around Mr. Mitchell and Mr. Cheney when I first came to work here."

Faye nodded her understanding. "You're a nice girl, Ella. Men like and respect girls like you. You're the kind of girl they want to marry. "

Ella smiled gratefully at Faye, then stood and smoothed her hair. "I think I'll be all right now. Do I look awful?"

"You look fine. Let me run a comb through your hair and put some lipstick on you. You'll be as good as new."

This done, they walked together through the warehouse. Faye put her arm around Ella. *I shouldn't judge others too quickly. I don't know what's in their heart. Only God knows that.*

Just before they entered the office area, Faye squeezed Ella's shoulder and walked back to her own duties. Ella returned to her desk.

Billie looked at her sympathetically but said nothing. Ella was grateful, for she was afraid if anyone spoke to her now she'd burst into fresh tears.

She went back to the calculator. Mr. Mitchell had checked her computations and two of the invoices were incorrect. He had corrected her figures in red pencil. Mr. Mitchell always checked the invoices both before and after they were typed to prevent them from going out with errors.

At last the long day was over and she was free to leave.

"Good night," she bade Nita, and clocked out.

"Good night." She smiled at Ella, but there was sadness in her smile.

Time rolled around, and soon Ella had been working for Economy Textiles for more than two years. She wanted to always work at this company with the girls with whom she felt so close.

But it was not to be. The next day Mr. Richardson met with Mr. Cheney and Mr. Mitchell for over two hours. It was nearing lunchtime when the meeting broke up and the men came out.

Mr. Richardson made the announcement. "We will soon be going through the process of shutting down this plant. You are free to look for jobs elsewhere; however, we will try to place you at Stone Manufacturing Company if there's an opening."

Ella felt a deep loyalty to the company and didn't want to think about working anywhere else. She felt she belonged here with the people she'd worked with and of whom she'd become so fond.

It's like leaving a sinking ship and I'm the last one to get into the lifeboat.

That evening she told Doris the news. "It's like I'm leaving them in the lurch."

But Doris commented sensibly, "Your first duty is to yourself. You'll have to look for another job. You don't owe them anything."

Ella couldn't seem to get across to Doris the sense of loyalty she had. She knew she'd need another job soon, but it was hard to say goodbye to her first job and the girls with whom she'd worked.

We've been like sisters. What will I do without them?

Soon they'd have to part. Each would go her separate way, but she would always remember them as special people. Faye was especially important to Ella. She was grateful for the close relationship they'd shared. She knew because of that relationship she could now walk more confidently into the future that awaited her.

Farewells must come, but also must come new greetings.

ONE DANCE

Judy noticed him soon after the first dance class began held for the beginning junior hostesses at the USO club. She and her older sister and friend had joined when the club opened following the Korean War.

The duties of the junior hostesses were to express hospitality to the servicemen, serving as hatcheck girls, making milkshakes, and dispensing soft drinks and snacks at the snack bar. They were taught the fox trot, tango, rumba, mambo, polka, waltz, shag, and jitterbug to ensure that they could dance with the soldiers. Judy quickly learned the slower dances, but she had two left feet when it came to the shag and jitterbug.

There was more physical contact in the slower, more romantic dances and this contact made her feel safe. In dancing farther away from her partner, connected only by their joined hands as required in the shag and jitterbug, she would have felt "on stage" – exposed.

Her need to feel sheltered was met if the man had a strong lead, because then she could rely on him to guide her. This confidence in his ability to lead left her free to enjoy the dance. If her partner held her close to him she could anticipate his next step, and thus avoid an awkward move to throw them off balance.

A man's confident self-assurance attracted her to him and heightened her enjoyment. It allowed her to move with him in a smooth rhythm that pleased them both. The joy of being able to instinctively follow a man's lead gave her the illusion that they belonged to each other for those brief moments, and her pleasure was complete if he expressed his appreciation with a smiling, "You're a very good dancer!"

The airman who had first caught her interest approached the dance class one evening while she and the other girls were watching their exuberant instructor demonstrate the quick steps of the shag, as easily as if she were twenty instead of past her forties.

Judy's eyes registered his slight build as he neared the group, white shirt sleeves rolled to the elbow, contrasting sharply with a dark complexion, khakis clinging to a narrow waist and slender hips and legs. Although his physique was slim a wiry strength was in evidence, manifested by his corded arms and strong neck below a head full of dark hair, slightly longer than the average serviceman's. All created a fascinating picture for her captured gaze.

Heart beating erratically in excitement and fear, she sat down before he got near enough to conduct conversation, bending over in pretense of tying her shoe.

Through her lashes, her upward glance revealed a slightly aquiline nose, dark eyes, and black hair-- giving witness to his Latin heritage. He stood silently watching the girls with their instructor. Taking a deep draw on his cigarette, he slowly exhaled. The smoke drifted up to encircle his head, and his eyes narrowed to avoid it, seeming to add to his attractiveness. Pretending to work on her other shoe, she saw him saunter over to the snack bar. When she raised herself up she saw that he had taken a seat to order some refreshment.

She worked the hatcheck desk on Tuesday nights, so she was free to attend the dances on Friday nights. If an emergency came up to prevent a girl from being at work on her regular night, whether it be Tuesday or Friday, she could call the Director of Activities, explain her dilemma and make up the hours later.

She found herself looking for him on Friday nights, and her heart would leap at seeing the sleek dark head, inevitable white shirt, sleeves rolled to the elbow, and khaki pants. There seemed to be an elusiveness about him that set him apart, making him that much more mysterious and fascinating.

From the hat check desk facing the front entrance she could easily see those arriving. Usually she was kept busy taking the girls' sweaters or jackets or the men's jackets, and caps, if they had worn one, but, in the lulls between the rush she could observe part of the crowd, and overhear bits of conversation drifting her way now and then.

On this Tuesday Judy saw him enter the Club with a couple of other servicemen.

His voice, that she managed to overhear, was deep and husky, almost raspy—*probably from the cigarettes.*

Then came a Friday night when the crowd was scarce and only a few girls were working. It seemed to be an off night all way around, so Judy took a cup of fruit punch from the snack bar, and sat down while things were slow. She took a sip, as she watched with interest one particular couple dancing, a husband and wife team who were very good together. They were presently engaged in a lively polka in which they excelled, and were just as proficient in the shag.

Her lips lifted in a smile at their obvious enjoyment, wondering how feet could move so fast, especially as the girl wore high heels. Absorbed in watching the couple directly before her she failed to see the figure approaching from the sidelines, the dark hair and eyes, white shirt with sleeves rolled up to the elbow, the khaki pants which fit closely to his graceful form.

She looked up to see a hand reaching out to her in an unspoken invitation to dance. Disbelieving her eyes, she sat frozen to her seat for a moment. He'd never seemed to see her, had never asked her for a dance, always choosing a livelier, more popular dance partner. Looking silently up into his dark, velvety eyes, she set her punch cup down on the table next to the sofa and stood slowly, not trusting her legs to support her. Unsteadily, she took a step forward to take his hand and he held her close to him, so that with her hand on his shoulder her forehead rested against his hard warm cheek.

Dreamily, she began moving with him, the music uniting them as they swayed in perfect synchronization to its rhythm.

Her feet never hesitated or faltered, for he was the perfect dance partner, having a strong lead. His hand pressing her closely against him enabled her to anticipate his next step, and they moved in total harmony. Wishing to drift along with him forever with the warmth of his face against hers, and her body close to his warm one; nevertheless, she remembered the lessons the USO girls had been taught: "Junior hostesses are expected to be hospitable!"

So she felt compelled to break the spell, and lifting her head away from his, she spoke, her voice breathless from his nearness. "Where are you from?"

The question was not an unusual one as there were servicemen at the nearby base who were from every corner of the globe.

"My parents emigrated from Puerto Rico to the Bronx in New York City, so I grew up there," his pleasant, husky voice replied.

"I've lived here all my life. I suppose it must be difficult to adjust to a new country."

He shrugged his shoulders negligently.

"I learned to speak English at school. It wasn't too bad."

"Oh, good."

Then, knowing nothing else to say she let her forehead lean against his cheek once more. It felt so right, as if she had always known how it would feel to be held in his arms, their bodies blending together to the music. The tune changed on the jukebox, and without missing a step he led her into the next song.

His breath smelled faintly of tobacco, but strangely it was not offensive. She could feel the scratchy beginning of his beard against her face, and it felt so natural, so dear to have her cheek against his.

"Oh—I'm Judy Wilcox," she spoke into his ear, suddenly realizing that she and he did not know one another's name.

"Jose' Montez," he introduced himself.

They seemed to fit together so perfectly, and her feet never hesitated in following his steps to a smooth foxtrot. They swayed to the music—then he turned her around easily, still holding her close to him as they continued to move as one. She felt as if they were one entity, mentally as well as physically. He seemed to exert a magnetic pull that enthralled her with their closeness, aided by the romantic mood set by the music emanating from the jukebox. She felt the sweetness from the closeness of his body against hers that she couldn't explain, even to herself, because it was indescribable. She only knew a wordless joy that she didn't question but only savored. Then the song ended and they broke apart.

He led her back to the sofa, where she'd been sitting when he'd invited her to dance. Again she tried to engage him in conversation, but the magic was gone. He answered her attentively when she inquired about his family, but she could feel his interest palling. "Excuse me," he spoke politely, as he stood and crushed his cigarette into the ashtray on the table beside her.

Feeling a kind of grief, she realized the deep emotion she'd thought they'd shared had been hers only. She sensed that he was like an elusive butterfly that could not be captured, but must remain unhampered in its need to fly wherever it chose.

She had to let him go, but she was fiercely glad they'd shared this time—one perfect moment, one perfect dance. It would be hers to treasure, to hold always in her heart. Only one dance, but one she would remember forever.

AFRAID TO LOVE

Olivia sat watching the couples swaying back and forth. She observed their animated faces and listened to the hum of their flirty conversations despite the press of the dancers around them on the crowded dance floor.

"Hi! Is this seat reserved?"

Olivia looked up to see a rather short, blonde young man with thick glasses gesturing to the empty seat next to her. She could barely hear him over the pandemonium from the dance floor and the music from the jukebox.

"No. Please have a seat. Isn't the noise awful?"

"Sure is! This is my first time here. You must be one of the Junior Hostesses from the USO Club I've been hearing about from some of the guys on base."

"Yep, I'm a Junior Hostess. I was just taking a break from the hatcheck desk, which is where I usually work on Tuesday and Saturday nights, or the snack bar if needed."

"Well, I always wear "civvies" into town when I get a chance instead of my monkey suit. That's what we call our uniforms. By the way, I'm Glenn Havird."

His hair was a light reddish-blonde, his eyes a gray-blue with equally light eyebrows and eyelashes. His features weren't that outstanding, but his pleasant personality and wide smile made up for his lack of good looks.

"I'm Olivia Waters," she smiled, as she reached out to take his outstretched hand. She moved over to allow room for him to sit beside her.

"Where are you from?" she asked as he joined her on the sofa.

"A small town near Fort Wayne, Indiana. Did you know that Indiana got its name from the word Indian? How about the fact that we sell a lot of farm products but have industrial production as well; or the forests Indiana has are important because of the large variety of trees? I learned that from the study of state history required to graduate from high school."

Leaning his arm on the back of the sofa, he turned to face her and changed the subject abruptly. "How old are you?"

Somehow she didn't take offence at what could be considered a personal question. "I was twenty-one on August 17."

"I just turned twenty in June."

"So I'm a little over a year older than you."

"I don't think an age difference matters. David, my friend over there is 29, and we get along okay." He nodded his head at a dark-headed, slender man sitting on a stool at the jam-packed snack bar.

"I have a sister here somewhere. She's four years older than I but I don't see her right now."

"We'll have to get David and her together and double-date sometime. David is a little reserved and hasn't made many friends here yet."

"That would be nice," Olivia agreed. She was normally hesitant about getting too familiar with the servicemen at the nearby Air Force Base, but she liked his outgoing personality and down home manner. Although he was clearly an extrovert, there was also something in his eyes that told her he had a serious side. Her woman's intuition told her he was an honest and sincere young man.

"Hey, David is headed this way. He must have seen me. David, over here!" He made a small megaphone with his hands and shouted loudly over the crowd to be heard.

David soon grew near enough for conversation and Glenn introduced him to Olivia.

"Olivia was just telling me her older sister is here somewhere."

Just then Olivia spotted her sister through the mob and caught her attention, motioning Jessica to join them. Jessica managed to make her way through the crush to where her sister and Glenn were seated. David and Glenn stood as Jessica approached.

"David, Glenn, this is my sister, Jessica."

Jessica gave them a hesitant smile and shook their extended hands. Jessica was more cautious in her relationships than Olivia. She felt that Olivia still needed her protection, despite the only four-year difference between them.

"Hey, why don't we make up a foursome and go out for pizza?" suggested Glenn.

"Fine with me," agreed David. The two girls gave their consent. The noise and milling bodies were wearing on their nerves, and the thought of escaping the crush and the loud rock and roll music from the jukebox was a welcome one.

David and Glenn had shared a ride in David's dark sedan. As the young people walked to the car they felt revived by the fresh evening air. Glenn kept them all laughing with his wise cracks, and they all got into the car. Olivia fell in with Glenn's silly mood. They all kept a lively repartee going as they drove to their next destination. They arrived at Capri's restaurant, which was famous for its pizza, and they hit it off so well they planned a trip to the nearby mountains for the next afternoon after they all attended Sunday services at the girls' church. Olivia and Jessica would prepare a picnic basket to carry along for their trip.

They left promptly at one. The cool morning had developed into a warm afternoon, and Olivia regretted not changing from her long-sleeved blouse and wool skirt into something cooler.

"Wow, look at the color of those leaves!" Glenn exclaimed as they neared the heart of the mountains where the brilliant hues of oak and maple trees contrasted with the background of dark green pines. They stopped and parked the car at the next overlook and climbed out to take in the breathtaking view.

"Sassafras Mountain, at 3,560 feet, is our tallest mountain." Olivia told Glenn.

"Our highest point in Indiana is 1,253 feet. We have one of the largest caves in the United States, Wyandotte Cave," he replied. "Really?" Olivia asked, her face full of surprise.

David spoke up, "I'm from Vermont so this reminds me a little of my own state." He sounded a little nostalgic and the girls glanced at him in silent sympathy. "There's supposed to be one overlook where you can see a part of three different states," Jessica declared. She and David found a large rock to sit on and relaxed, while Glenn and Olivia strolled a little farther to the protective rail near the edge of the drop-off.

Olivia fanned her face with her hand and said, "I guess you could say this is Indian summer weather."

"So you know what Indian summer is?"

"Yes, it's a name for the time of year when there's a warm spell after the first frost. It's a reminder that autumn is on its way out and winter is coming."

"Hey, you got it right! Some people don't know that. It feels like summer today."

David and Jessica approached Glenn and Olivia, and David asked, "Are you two about ready to eat? I'm starving!"

"You and me, both!" agreed Glenn.

They walked back to the car and the girls brought out the picnic basket. David lifted it onto the hood and they used it as a table.

"I smell fried chicken." Glenn sniffed appreciatively at the aromas wafting up from the container. They all filled their plates with the bounty of food, and everyone was soon eating hungrily.

"I think someone is a pretty good cook," remarked David around a bite of his ham biscuit.

"You're right there, my friend. Say, did you bring your camera? I went off and forgot mine," said Glenn, hitting himself on the forehead in mock self-punishment.

"Yes. Complete with a new roll of film."

"Well, you can take all the pictures you want but save a shot for Olivia. I want one of her by herself," said Glenn, with a wink at her. Olivia flushed with embarrassment but was secretly pleased and flattered that Glenn wanted a picture of her. David began snapping shots of the beautiful scenery and different poses of the group, saving the last shot for Olivia. After he'd used up the roll of film, he rewound it and put it in the protective case to avoid exposure.

The girls packed up the leftovers, while Glenn and David strolled back for a last view of the overlook, and David enjoyed a cigarette. They returned to the car and Glenn remarked, "I'm relieved we'll be going down the mountain this time!" Everyone laughed, but Olivia was a little tense. She often became carsick going down the sharp curves of the mountain. Fortunately, David drove at a moderate speed so she felt only her ears pop a little due to the difference in atmospheric pressure.

The four of them double-dated several more times but it wasn't long before they paired off with David and Jessica going out together, and Glenn dating Olivia.

Glenn had run across a pretty good used car of which he was very proud. Olivia complimented him on finding one that wasn't a lemon. She told him, "The used car salesmen around here are famous for taking advantage of the servicemen."

Glenn took Olivia out for pizza again at Capri's. Olivia told Glenn, "I went to school with Guide Capri. His family owns the two restaurants, and you'd never guess that he's Italian because he's blonde with fair skin and blue eyes. He explained to a teacher who had asked him about it that his family originated from one of the islands off the coast of Italy whose residents were fair-skinned and blue-eyed."

"No kidding!" He remarked.

Just then the waiter brought them the menu. After a glance at it Glenn ordered for them. "Two mushroom pizzas and two cokes, please."

The Italian pizza pie was brought back from overseas by some of the returning servicemen who'd developed a taste for it. When their order was received the sliced mushrooms looked very large to Olivia.

"Here, roll it up like this, starting at the point and rolling it up toward the crust," instructed Glenn, who had seen that she was having difficulty in handling her first slice. After that she had no difficulty in managing her pizza and enjoyed the tart tomato flavor, the stringy mozzarella cheese, and the tasty mushrooms.

Glenn shared with her that the airmen basic, airmen third, and airmen second rank of servicemen did not receive a large salary.

"After making my car payment and taking my uniforms to the laundry, I don't have much left. Thank goodness I can eat for free in the mess hall and sleep in the barracks!" he said, giving her a rueful smile.

They had finished their pizza and were preparing to leave the restaurant. Glenn held her coat for her, and she slipped her arms into the sleeves and smiled him her appreciation.

"Well, we can always go to my apartment and watch television," offered Olivia as they walked hand in hand toward Glenn's parked car.

"Say, that sounds great! It is sure swell of you to offer, Olivia. I might just take you up on that," Glenn remarked, opening the car door for her. She slid onto the seat and he closed the door.

As she watched him walk around to the driver's side, she reflected that it probably was difficult for a young soldier to make his pay stretch, especially if he had a family. But if that were the case, she supposed he would receive more money.

"Do you have to send money home to help your parents?" she asked, as he reached to put the key into the ignition. She remembered overhearing a couple of soldiers discussing having to send money home each month to help parents in difficult circumstances.

"No, they're doing pretty well. Dad raises hogs to sell at the cattle sales and saves one occasionally to butcher for Mom and him. They do okay."

He turned into the driveway to the duplex apartment Olivia shared with Jessica, and Olivia realized that she was seeing a more serious side of Glenn's nature.

Many of their earlier dates had been shared with another of Glenn's friends, simply known as "Olie." Olie had the typical Swedish coloring: ruddy complexion, blue eyes, and pale blonde hair. He was nice in a quiet sort of way, and paired with Glenn's usual exuberance they complemented each other's personalities. She liked Olie, but it had left little time for just Glenn and herself. But tonight, they had been on their own.

Glenn shut off the car motor. The yard light shone on his face allowing Olivia to see his still features and intent expression. He started at her for a moment before reaching to turn on the ignition key.

"I'll call you tomorrow night," he told her as the engine caught. Puzzled, Olivia opened the car door and climbed out. After closing the door she threw up her hand in silent farewell and watched him back out of the driveway. Frowning slightly, she realized what had been different about the evening. Glenn usually came around to open the door for her and walk her to the front door. He hadn't done that tonight.

Shrugging her shoulders, she opened the door and entered the apartment.

Jessica was home, and Olivia hung up her coat and walked to the open door of the bathroom where her sister was brushing her teeth.

"Have a good evening?" Olivia asked her lightly. Jessica rinsed her mouth and dried her face on the towel before answering.

"Yes, it was nice. We stayed here and watched *The Hit Parade* and then played some Scrabble. David liked my cake." Jessica was a good cook and enjoyed baking cakes, continually trying new recipes, and she served a new one tonight.

"Good. I thought it was delicious myself. Are you and David an item?" she teased. Jessica shrugged, but Olivia noted the warm glow in her expression.

Jessica and David had dated one another for the past couple of months and from all indications they seemed to be getting serious. The girls finished their nightly preparations without saying too much, but Olivia was glad Jessica was pleased with the relationship developing between her and David.

After all Jessica was twenty-five and probably wishing for her own home and family. Olivia had been with Jessica so long she'd never questioned their circumstances, but it was time that Jessica thought of marriage.

Glenn did call Olivia the next evening and, as it was still early, she invited him to eat leftover fried chicken and banana sandwiches for Sunday night supper. He looked appreciatively at the plate she brought to the living room. They ate their meal in front of the television, and then Olivia took their dishes back into the kitchen. She returned to the living room and sat down by Glenn on the sofa.

"Thank you," he said, looking into her eyes. Then he took her chin in his fingers and kissed her. It was the first time he'd attempted to kiss her, and she felt the timing was perfect. They'd been seeing each other for two months now. It was the first time she'd been kissed by a man despite her twenty-one years.

Glenn did not draw away from her but continued to kiss her, his lips firm and hard against hers. Her heartbeat accelerated and, much to her embarrassment, she began to feel nauseated from having just eaten and the excitement of his kissing her before her food had settled. Getting up hastily, she said over her shoulder, managing to smile lightly. "Excuse me just a minute."

She left the room, closing the door behind her. She reached the bathroom just in time, but to her consternation she had soiled her dress. Jessica came in to see about her, and Olivia explained with a shrug, "I guess something must have disagreed with me." She ignored Jessica's look of surprise.

After changing into a blouse and skirt, she washed her face with a cool washcloth and repaired her make up. When she returned to the living room she said in apology, "I'm sorry. Something must have upset my stomach." Glenn responded dryly, "So I make you sick, do I?"

She demurred and turned her attention to the television. A few minutes later, she said, "It wasn't you, you know."

"What?"

"That made me sick. It was the banana. It was too ripe. I only like them when they're still a bit green. If they're too ripe they make me sick every time. I should have known better than to eat it."

"Oh. So you're okay now?"

"Yes."

"Also, you're the first man to kiss me. I am not used to feeling such exciting emotion, Glenn. It took me by surprise, and I couldn't handle it. Do you understand?"

In answer Glenn reached over and drew Olivia close to him, leaving his arm around her. He put his other hand into the opening of her shirtwaist blouse and slipped it under the edge of her bra, caressing the top of her breast.

The intimacy of the situation that had developed between them seemed so natural that she did not pull away from him, but continued to let him hold her and stroke her skin. His action made her feel protected and secure. To her, it was far more than a sexual advance. Looking into his blue eyes, she felt a sincerity radiating from him that convinced her he cared about her. She felt an unspoken tenderness in him that soothed her and filled her with a feeling of completeness. She took comfort from the warmth of his hand, his arm wrapped around her and his body close to hers.

"Okay, now?" he asked, looking into her face with a new seriousness that she'd never seen in him, but one that she liked very much. She nodded, and they returned their attention to the television. They watched the rest of the *Ed Sullivan Show* and then the *Loretta Young Show* came on. He continued to caress her breast, and he kissed her again from time to time. His breath held the fragrance of the Spearmint chewing gum that he usually carried with him and shared with her. She caught a whiff of his aftershave lotion, an aroma that seemed his alone and one she'd never forget.

Glenn continued to ask Olivia out or they'd stay at her apartment to watch television. One particular evening they left the USO Club and he invited her to stop at an all-night diner for a piece of pie and coffee. He selected apple and she chose cherry. As she cut into the limp crust and tart filling, Glenn asked her, "Have you ever thought about marrying a soldier?"

Since she had never seriously debated marrying anyone, even a serviceman, she answered him honestly. "No, I haven't." He didn't comment further but his expression was thoughtful, as if it was a subject that had been on his mind for some time.

Olivia was so inexperienced and unsure of herself it didn't occur to her that he may have been leading up to a marriage proposal. Neither of them pursued the subject and Olivia soon forgot his question.

It had become his habit to pull up in front of her apartment at the end of an evening and turn off the car lights. There was little illumination from the distant streetlight, but the porch light to her apartment afforded enough light for them to see one another's faces. Glenn would then pull her close and kiss her, often studying her face intently and saying quietly, "I want you," or at other times, "I love you."

Then he'd ask her, "Do you want me?" She felt uncomfortable, and usually nodded her head just because she wanted to please him, and felt this was what he wished her to say. Having no understanding, in her naiveté, what the term, "I want you," meant she was unmoved by his declaration.

"Say it," he would coax, either "I love you," or "I want you." She would repeat the words to satisfy him, but they felt stiff and unfamiliar on her lips, and meant nothing to her.

Christmas was approaching and the USO planned its annual Christmas dance. Olivia decided to splurge and buy a new dress instead of having one made. She selected a red taffeta because it was Christmas. The dress, with its rounded neck, short sleeves, and a large bow in the back at her waist, was very becoming. The full skirt and crinoline petticoat beneath emphasized her slender form, and Glenn took a couple of snapshots of her with his new Polaroid camera before they left for the dance. She enjoyed the dance, although Glenn was not a proficient dancer.

The music was good and refreshments appetizing so it was a very nice affair. On the nights they spent at her apartment in front of the television, Jessica would remain discreetly in the bedroom or kitchen. If she were home, she would close the living room off to give them some privacy.

Glenn invariably sat close to her with his arm around her, inserting his hand into the neckline of her blouse or dress, resting it on the top of her breast. The sexual overtones of the situation were lost to her. She savored only the feeling of being held closely in his arms that gave her a sense of warm security, and satisfied the desire she felt for affection.

He'd kiss her hard at times, and her heartbeat would accelerate, but any thought of carrying it further didn't occur to her. It was enough that he caressed her and looked into her eyes. She interpreted his expression as one of love and a sincere affection for her alone. The warm glow of emotional security, the feeling that she belonged to him and he to her satisfied her completely.

Gradually he began to grow bolder with his lovemaking, drawing her down to lie on the couch beside him and kissing her ardently. Then came the night he attempted to touch her intimately in a way no one had ever done—sliding his hand under her dress, his fingers seeking her under the edge of her panties.

Reflexively, her hand closed over his, resisting him with all her strength to prevent his fingers from probing further. His action repelled her. She felt that her personal being was being violated—that her body was hers and hers alone. No one was supposed to touch her there.

"It's just Nature," he tried to soothe her, but she was adamant in her rejection.

He sat up and looked at her with that serious, meaningful expression that seemed to embody his very self to her, that was so familiar and so dear.

"Maybe I'd just better leave," he said looking down at her gravely. She sensed that he'd felt hurt and rejected, like the boy, and yet the man. She took his arm and pulled him down beside her.

"Oh, come on. Sit back down."

Reluctantly, he did so but only for a few minutes. Then he told her he had to prepare for an upcoming barracks inspection. He'd explained what an ordeal that was—everything in the barracks was to be spotless, each bed made so that a quarter would bounce on it, their footlockers had to be lined up just so, their shoed shined to perfection. Nothing would be overlooked, not even the floors.

She also remembered that he was leaving soon to go home to Indiana for Christmas leave.

She walked him to the door, and he put his arm around her to kiss her goodnight, then left. It never occurred to her that it was normal sexual behavior for a man to want consummation of a relationship, that his arousal was more intense than her own. To her, his kisses meant affection and approval with no link to anything sexual. In fact, she had no idea how one went about it.

She'd been deprived of love and affection at an early age, and was still at the emotional level of a child. She wished only for the comfort of an uncomplicated relationship, one based on being held, caressed, and kisses with no alternate agenda. It was enough for her, and it never occurred to her that it wasn't for him.

As Christmas drew closer Olivia wanted to buy Glenn something special for his gift. She found a pretty tie and a nice pair of socks to match the plain gray suit he'd worn when he and David had attended church services with Jessica and her. The set cost more than she'd planned on spending, but she liked it and couldn't wait until she could give it to him and see his surprised expression.

But that evening she was in for a surprise of her own.

When she entered the apartment from work that afternoon Jessica was home, and Olivia saw immediately from her red, swollen eyes that she'd been crying.

"What happened?" Jessica almost never cried, so she knew it had to be something very serious.

"D-David is married. He told me just now when he stopped by after work."

"But why did he wait so long to tell you?"

"He had to tell me, because he's being transferred to a base in New Zealand, and his wife is going with him," replied Jessica bitterly.

"Oh, Jessica, I'm so sorry," Olivia said, taking Jessica's arm and leading her to sit down beside her on the bed.

"You're sorry! How do you think I feel? I was beginning to fall in love with him, and thought he returned my feelings. Men! There's not a one you can trust as far as you can throw him," she spat derisively.

Olivia looked at Jessica's face in alarm. Jessica was always the calm one, always so in control. She never let anything upset her, and never showed her feelings. Olivia realized that Jessica had been deeply scarred by her experience with David, and that she wouldn't get over it so easily.

Not knowing what to say, Olivia sat silently patting Jessica's arm. Wordlessly, Jessica stood and began getting ready for bed. Olivia did the same, her thoughts in turmoil. *How could have this happened to Jessica? She was always so level headed, always knew the right thing to do, and her judgment was usually so impeccable!*

Olivia realized the following morning that Jessica was still bitter, perhaps even more so.

"Are you going out with Glenn tonight?" Jessica asked her, disapproval in her expression.

Jessica had never objected to Olivia's dating Glenn, but she saw that Jessica was turning her hurt and betrayal toward Glenn because he and David were friends.

"H-He's only stopping by for a few minutes. He's going home for Christmas and wanted to bring my gift."

"What did you get him?" Jessica looked at her with eyes filled with pain and defeat.

"A tie and a pair of socks. I was just getting ready to wrap them."

Hesitantly, she held the box out for Jessica's approval. Jessica fingered the tie and examined the socks.

"They're nice. I bet you paid a lot for them," she muttered darkly.

"They are just what I was looking for," Olivia said happily, then regretted her statement as she looked at Jessica's wan expression.

"It would have to happen at Christmas," Jessica mourned, her arms wrapped around herself.

"I'm so sorry, Jessica." She felt she didn't know this new Jessica, how to treat her, or how to talk to her. Olivia felt that Jessica was thinking: "Oh, I guess I'll get over it. I'll have to. I'll have to because I have to take care of you!"

Olivia looked down at the gift box she still held. "Well, I guess I'll have to wrap this before he gets here," she said, turning away in embarrassment, not wanting Jessica to see the hurt in her eyes. Her excitement about Glenn's gift was dimmed now, but she had to wrap it anyway. Olivia had just finished tying the ribbon when the doorbell rang.

She heard Jessica close the door to the living room with a distinctive click as she hurried to answer the front door. A blast of cold air hit her as she opened the door to Glenn.

"Whew, it's chilly outside!" exclaimed Glenn as he entered the warm room.

"It feels like it."

She looked at him nervously. She didn't mentioned Jessica or David.

"Merry Christmas!" smiled Glenn, reaching out to take her hand. He placed the gift package he'd been hiding behind him into it. Olivia looked with shock at the clumsily wrapped package she'd instinctively taken from him.

"Merry Christmas to you," she smiled in reply, handing him the gift that she'd wrapped with such care. They sat down on the sofa to unwrap their gifts. Olivia let him open her gift to him first, watching for his expression when he saw what was inside. He smiled and kissed her.

"Do you like it?" she asked with doubt in her eyes.

"It's very nice," he answered, putting his arm around her and hugging her to him. "After I bought my round trip bus ticket for home, and left myself some Christmas money for my parents, I didn't have very much money left," he said apologetically, watching her remove the wrapping paper from his gift to her. She was speechless when she saw what the package held. It was a tawdry gift box of powder and cologne, "Evening in Paris," which could be purchased cheaply at any of the dime stores.

"Oh, h-how lovely." Her cheeks burned hot with humiliation. She knew it was supposed to be the thought that counted, but she was sick with disappointment after the care and money with which she'd selected his gift.

"I didn't know what to get you, so the salesclerk suggested it," he explained diffidently.

"It's very nice," she responded with false enthusiasm.

"Well, say, I'd better hustle. I've got to help the guys get the barracks ready for inspection tomorrow, then I'll be leaving tomorrow evening to go home for the holidays."

Holding his gift from her in one hand, he hugged her to him again and gave her a quick kiss. His face was still cool from the cold air outside, and she smelled his familiar cologne.

"Have a nice Christmas," she said, trying hard to smile.

"You, too. Wish you the best. I'll call you when I get back. Remember I'm only staying a week."

Then he was gone, and she slowly closed the door and sat down on the sofa. She looked up as Jessica opened the door and entered the living room. Jessica saw the "Evening in Paris" box in Olivia's lap and lifted her eyebrows in distaste.

"He didn't give you much, did he?" she remarked sarcastically.

Olivia suddenly burst into tears and fled into the bathroom, closing the door behind her and locking it. She lowered the commode seat and sat down, sobbing as if her heart would break. *How could Glenn have done it?* She felt as if she would never stop crying, her disappointment overwhelming her, and that his gift had been a measure of his regard for her.

The next few days seemed to drag by for Olivia. Jessica's mood hadn't changed—she still remained bitter and unforgiving—and it made Olivia feel depressed and unsure of herself. She couldn't help but wonder if Glenn knew when he'd introduced Jessica to him that David Winters was a married man. There had been rumors at the USO Club about married men getting involved with the Junior Hostesses on occasion, and perhaps Olivia and Jessica had not taken them seriously enough, thinking them too improbable.

The men were from many different states and from many foreign countries, and had traveled all over the world during their tours of duty. Who knew what they had done, or where their travels had taken them? What was the old saying--Out sight, out of mind? She'd heard that the percentage of failed marriages for servicemen was high. The life was very hard on the wives and families of the military, no matter what rank they held.

An incident that had happened soon after Olivia met Glenn came to mind. The series of events flashed through her mind as she sat staring with unseeing eyes at the television screen. Glenn had come over right after lunch one Sunday afternoon, bringing with him some snapshots he'd taken while stationed in Korea.

She recalled his every word and expression as he had shown them to her, as well as her feelings of shock and revulsion. Several of the photographs were of prostitutes. She'd stared silently at those snapshots of the bar girls and wondered how Glenn happened to be with them, and why he'd taken their photographs. He'd explained, "There's nothing else for them to do. They have to make a living for themselves."

Olivia tried not to judge them too harshly. After all, she'd told herself, she'd never experienced being in a war-torn country and couldn't imagine what the circumstances were that led these girls to such a degrading occupation But was it necessary for Glenn to take pictures of them to bring home with him? And worse still, why did he have to show them to her?

The sharp ring of the telephone aroused her from her reverie. She picked up the receiver and said absently, "Hello," still caught up in her memories of that afternoon, and uncertain of what they meant.

"Hi! How are you, Olivia? So Glenn was back from Indiana.

"Oh, I guess I'm fine. And you?"

"Oh, great. Are you busy? May I come over?"

"Uh, sure. You can tell me all about your holiday at home," she answered, managing to inject some enthusiasm into her voice.

"See you in a bit, then."

While she waited for him to arrive she examined her feelings. For one thing, she was nervous after what had transpired between Jessica and David, and wondered again if Glenn was aware of it. Should she ask Glenn about it, and find out once and for all if he'd known from the beginning that David was married?

All too soon, it seemed, the doorbell rang. Jessica had gone with a girl from work to a musical concert, so Olivia had to answer the door. She was glad that Jessica had gotten out and hoped the operetta would cheer her up. Taking a deep breath to fortify herself she opened the door. To her surprise she was glad to see Glenn. It was as if he'd never been away.

"Come in."

Glenn took her hand and she led him to the sofa. As soon as they were seated he gazed at with his own unique expression of silent appraisal, as if he were trying to look into her mind and read her thoughts, see into her very heart.

"Did you enjoy your Christmas at home?" she asked trying to sound casual and at ease, although her heart was beating erratically.

"Yeah, it was okay. There's this girl who lives next door to me. She's written me regularly, and it was like she was trying to get too serious—like she owned me. It got me kind of fed up with her," he told her, his words and expression registering irritation.

Olivia didn't know what to say so she waited, uncertain whether to comment on the situation and if so, how. Mercifully, he unzipped his jacket and pulled out two phonograph records. "I brought you a little something," he told her almost shyly. She took the records and looked at the titles. "Would you like to hear them?"

"Sure, why not?" she agreed.

He took the records over to the console desk that held the record player, the desk that Olivia's aunt had given to her and Jessica. He opened up the top of the machine and put both records on, but it could hold ten records at once. After one record had played the next one dropped down automatically. Jessica and she had enjoyed the record player very much and were beginning to start their own small collection of favorites.

The strains of Roger Williams' piano rendition of *Autumn Leaves* followed by Gogi Grant's vocal, *It's Just the Nearness of You* soon were heard. Olivia knew at that moment that she would always associate these two songs with Glenn.

"Do you like them?" he asked eagerly.

"Oh, yes. I like them both!"

One thing she could thank Jessica for was instilling in her an appreciation for music, both popular and the semi-classics. While they were relaxed together, Olivia suddenly decided to ask Glenn if he knew that David Winters was married.

"Glenn"…she paused, to gather her thoughts and choose her words carefully. "Jessica told me that David Winters has confessed to her that he is married."

She glanced at him to see what his expression would reveal.

"Married! Well, if you think I knew about it, you'd better think again!" he exclaimed in anger and surprise.

"It's only natural that Jessica and I would wonder," she said defensively.

Glenn put his arm around her and drew her close. He sighed deeply before saying,

"Look, Olivia. I've seen so many guys come and go I've learned not to get close to any of them because I know, chances are, they'll get shipped out and I'll never see them again. I try not to even remember their names. David and I haven't known each other very long, or very well. I've also learned not to ask questions. Can you understand that?"

He looked honestly into her eyes, and she had to believe him.

"Yes, I think I can, but Jessica had pretty much fallen in love with him before he told her. He's being transferred to New Zealand, and taking his wife with him. Now she's heartbroken, moping around and snapping at everyone in her path."

"Oh, gosh, I'm so sorry, Olivia. That really is too bad. I had no idea. David and I have gone out for a beer occasionally, been bowling a couple of times, and the night we met you and Jessica was the first time either of us had been to the USO Club. He and Olie are about the only guys I know by name, and that's only because we are in the same barracks.

They came to the base a few months ago—Olie first, and then David about a month afterwards. I've only been here since July so we're all basically newcomers. Most guys stay a year or longer, some not that long.

When you enlist they give you three choices of where you want to go. Everybody tells you to put down the place you want to be stationed as your last choice, because they usually send you to your first pick. So if your choose Texas or California first, they'll probably send you somewhere on the East Coast, or the South. That's just how the military operates," he explained earnestly.

Olivia nodded, listening to every word. Every nuance of his expression told her he was telling the truth.

"I guess it's just one of those things," she sighed, her eyes now on the hands clasped in her lap. "I don't suppose anything you could say to Jessica would do much good. It wouldn't really change anything that's happened. I don't think she'd believe you, anyway. She's just so bitter and withdrawn-- not like herself at all. It scares me."

He squeezed her shoulders in sympathy, and then glanced at his watch.

"Well, it's getting late. Jessica will probably be home before long. I don't think it will help any for her to see me, so I'd better go."

He stood up and they walked to the door together, his arm still holding her close to him. He kissed her lightly on her nose, cuffed her playfully under the chin, and opened the door.

"I'll call you tomorrow to see how things are going," he promised, as he closed the screened door between them.

"Okay. Goodnight, Glenn," she said, grateful that he'd helped allay her doubts.

He gave her a mock salute as he turned to walk away, and she closed the door, leaving the front porch light on for Jessica.

Olivia must have been asleep when Jessica came in. When she awoke, she looked over at the other twin bed. Jessica's was made up, and her clothes were laid out for the day. She knew that Jessica would be in the kitchen preparing breakfast for the two of them.

Throwing back her cover, Olivia, too, got up and pulled on her housecoat over her warm flannel pajamas. It felt chilly in the apartment and she knew the weather outside must have turned colder during the night.

In the kitchen, Olivia felt the inviting warmth of the small gas space heater in the corner of the kitchen. She hovered around it for a brief moment, glancing at her pet parakeet in his cage on top of the hot water heater next to the stove.

Although the parakeet was Olivia's, given to her by the first boy she'd dated just out of high school, it was Jessica who gave him most of the attention and care. She kept fresh paper in his birdcage, provided him with birdseed and water, and whistled to him in an effort to encourage him to talk.

Olivia had dated Bobby for over a year. He was tall and heavy, almost to the point of obesity, with dark hair and eyes, his face slightly scarred from teenage-suffered acne. He was quiet and rather shy. They'd usually get a hamburger and cola and go to a drive-in movie. Despite their long association, he'd never held her hand or attempted to kiss her.

They'd formed a comfortable friendship—sort of a relationship of habit. But when Olivia had met Glenn and they began dating each other, Olivia had told Bobby that she'd met someone else, and he'd asked her to go steady. Bobby had appeared relieved, his face breaking into a smile as, oddly enough, he'd also become involved with another girl with whom he wished to go steady.

He probably had hesitated to break up with Olivia, not knowing exactly how to go about it, and not wishing to hurt her feelings.

All this was going through Olivia's thoughts as she warmed herself by the heater, and the bird swung on his trapeze and pecked his oyster shell to get his calcium for the day. Smelling the tempting aroma of coffee, she looked at the meal that Jessica had prepared, ready in the breakfast nook that was tucked in the corner between the sink and the cabinets.

"Good morning. How was your evening?" she asked Jessica, sliding into one side of the booth and picking up her coffee from the small table between them.

"It was pretty good. The Furman Singers did *Naughty Marietta* and the orchestra sounded quite professional for a college performance," replied Jessica, her eyes absently studying the dripping faucet at the sink. Her expression was still withdrawn, but Olivia took hope that she was beginning to recover from the unhappy experience with David.

Jessica worked for a small short-line railroad where she'd been employed since completing high school. Prior to that, she had attended a business college for a short time to brush up on her shorthand and typing. She was good at her job, and seemed to like it.

Olivia hoped that the job Jessica enjoyed would help her recover from the hurt she was experiencing because of her unhappy relationship with David.

Olivia helped Jessica clear the table, and returned to the bedroom to make her bed and get ready for work. Her own job was with one of the nearby textile plants in the area. She, too, had gone to work out of high school, putting to use the typing and shorthand skills she'd learned from her business course at school.

"Glenn came over last night," she called to Jessica who was brushing her teeth. Jessica shut off the faucet and turned to wipe her face on the towel. Her expression tightened and she made no reply to Olivia's remark. Silently they each finished dressing. Jessica needed to leave first as she had to catch an earlier bus than Olivia.

"He said he'd call me tonight," she continued.

Jessica shrugged into her coat, grabbed her umbrella, and was ready to leave, slipping the strap of her bag over her shoulder.

"Bye," she said tersely as she went out the door, still not responding to Olivia's attempt at conversation.

That evening, Olivia and Jessica ate a quick supper of fish sticks, fresh creamed corn, sliced tomatoes with cucumbers, and brown and serve rolls. Quick as it was, Olivia thought it delicious. Jessica really was a fabulous cook. Since Jessica had cooked, Olivia did the dishes.

She was expecting Glenn to invite her out to a movie, or perhaps just a cup of coffee. Jessica settled down with the paper, and Olivia washed out a few personal things and hung them on the wooden clothes rack the girls used for drying small items of clothing. Then she did her nails and plucked her eyebrows, all the while listening with one ear for the telephone. The hour hand of the clock slowly moved around until it was nine o'clock.

Still Glenn hadn't called. Olivia glanced at Jessica, who was sewing some buttons on a blouse. They had come loose, although it was almost new, proving the point she'd often made that ready-made things were only half-finished nowadays.

As if feeling her glance, Jessica returned her look and pointedly eyed the clock.

"Didn't you say that Glenn promised to call tonight?"

She'd finally ended the silence that had stretched between them. Her voice and expression reflected her negative view toward Glenn and Olivia's relationship, and Olivia felt that Jessica was actually glad that Glenn hadn't called. It was as if his silence proved that he wasn't to be trusted.

Olivia nodded, her eyes on the magazine she'd picked up but hadn't read, and feeling miserable. The first chilly fingers of doubt crept down her spine. Glenn had told her he'd call but the phone remained silent. He rarely called this late, and her hopes were fading by the moment. Sick at heart, she leafed through her magazine, but her attention was not on its pages but on the disappointment that Glenn hadn't kept his promise. She glanced at the clock again. Nine-thirty. She now felt certain that he wouldn't call. Laying the magazine aside, she rose from the couch and muttered that she was going to take her bath.

She met Jessica's triumphant look that seemed to say, "I told you so."

Olivia's throat ached and her eyes moistened with unshed tears, but she didn't want Jessica to see them. She tried to put on a brave front, but it was an effort to do so.

Soon after Olivia was in bed, Jessica came through the bedroom to take her turn in the bathroom. Tossing restlessly, Olivia heard the water run into the tub and in a little while heard Jessica, too, preparing for bed.

She pretended to be asleep, her back turned to Jessica, and soon all was quiet. But sleep was far from her, and it was long after she heard the sleep-induced rhythm of Jessica's breathing before Olivia's eyes finally closed.

The girls had little to say the next morning as they ate breakfast and dressed for work. The sun was already bright, foretelling a nice day outside, but Olivia wasn't cheered by that fact. In fact, she still felt miserable and upset, with doubt and uncertainty drawing knots in her stomach. She felt a headache pressing at her temples as she combed her hair and applied her makeup. Jessica had already left for the bus stop, and Olivia knew she'd have to step on it to meet her own bus.

Somehow she made it through the day, and trudged slowly home from the bus stop. She was exhausted and still tense with worry. Sighing deeply she opened the door, bracing herself before she entered the apartment. She closed the door carefully behind her. *Surely Glenn would call tonight.*

She heard Jessica in the kitchen, knowing from the rattle of dishes and the closing of pot lids on the stove that she was preparing the evening meal. Olivia changed her clothes, lingering as long as she could before entering the kitchen. She wasn't hungry in the least, but she knew she had to go through the motions of pretending an appetite, even if it choked her to do so.

If not, Jessica would notice and it would give her further fuel to feed her conviction that Glenn wasn't true to his word and was untrustworthy. Olivia managed to eat enough to quell any of Jessica's suspicion that all was not well with her. She washed up as usual, and felt her stomach knot with anxiety as she put away the last glass and hung up the dishtowel. *Would he call tonight?*

She was polishing her work shoes when suddenly the phone pealed. Heart leaping into her throat she called to Jessica, "I'll get it!" With trembling fingers she picked up the receiver. "H-Hello," she managed to utter over the lump in her throat.

"Hi, Olivia," Glenn greeted her, his voice sounding as normal as ever. "Say, I'm sorry about not phoning last night; we had a squadron party and it was pretty mad around here. We had it in the mess hall, and by the time I made it back to the barracks it was pretty late. Then the phone was tied up. After that I knew you'd be in bed, and I didn't want to wake you. Are you mad at me?"

"No, that's okay. I had things to do, myself," she answered, trying to inject a casual lightness into her voice. "Did you have a good time?"

"Oh, it was okay. Some of the guys got pretty looped, throwing up and stuff. Guess you could say they tied one on. Drinking on an empty stomach does that to you. There were snacks so I ate some with my beer."

"Sounds like you were the smart one. I'm glad you didn't follow their example. You probably would've woke up with an awful headache," she teased. He'd never know how thankful she was!

"So, what are you doing tonight? Going to be busy?"

"No, not anything I can't postpone. What did you have in mind?"

"Well, I thought I'd come over for a while, if it's okay. Maybe we could play a few records or watch something on television."

"Fine by me. I'll make some popcorn and cocoa," she offered.

"Say, that sounds great! We didn't have much of a supper in the chow hall this evening. Liver! Yuck!" She knew liver was not one of his favorites.

"Glenn's coming over," she told Jessica, glad that she could help put to rest some of her own doubt and, hopefully, throw water on Jessica's pessimistic opinion of Olivia's relationship with Glenn. Not bothering to reply, Jessica gathered up her curlers and retired to the bathroom to shampoo her hair. Olivia went to the kitchen to make the popcorn and hot chocolate. She was rather proud of her hot chocolate, which she made from scratch preparing her syrup from cocoa, sugar, and hot water before adding it to the milk, as her mother always made it.

Her mother had been a good cook before she'd gotten sick. Now she was hospitalized again with the same problem she suffered with so often, a recurring severe depression. As she waited for the popcorn to finish popping, Olivia reminded herself she owed her mother a letter. She poured the popcorn into a bowl when it was ready and added melted butter and salt. She was reaching to get the cups and saucers from the cabinet when the doorbell rang. Hurrying to the door she opened it to Glenn.

"Come on in."

The night was much chillier than the sunny day had been. But that was typical for this time of year. She closed the door and ushered Glenn to a seat on the couch.

"I'll get the cocoa and popcorn," she said, starting toward the kitchen.

"Let me help," he offered, jumping up to follow her. She glanced at the bedroom, and breathed thankfully that Jessica was still doing her hair. Olivia gave Glenn the bowl of popcorn, then set the cups on a tray and poured the cocoa into a metal pitcher to keep it hot in case they wanted seconds.

"Wait. Let me carry the tray and you get the popcorn," Glenn insisted. "It's not as heavy as the tray."

"Why, thank you, sir," Olivia said lightly, pleased at his thoughtfulness. Just then Jessica came out of the bathroom with a comb and curler bag in her hand. She barely nodded her head at Glenn, who said in a rather surprised tone of voice, "Well, hello, Jessica. How are you?"

Hearing no reply, he hurried after Olivia into the living room and Olivia turned to shut the door behind him. Glenn jokingly pretended to shiver after he'd set the tray on the coffee table.

"Boy, did I get the cold shoulder!" he remarked, pretending to shiver again as he looked at her and grimaced.

"Yes, well, she's still very upset over what happened between her and David. It's soured her on all servicemen, I'm afraid."

"That's too bad."

They helped themselves to popcorn, serving it into smaller bowls from the larger one and taking a napkin to wipe their hands. "Ah, just the thing for a chilly night," Glenn sighed in appreciation. "And this cocoa tastes great. Do you have a special recipe?"

"No, not really. I just make it like Mother always made hers, with cocoa, sugar, hot water, and milk. You dissolve the sugar and cocoa in hot water before adding it to the milk, and that is your chocolate syrup. You don't get all the lumps," she explained with a grin.

"Wow, that's really using the old noodle."

She smiled at his compliment. "Would you like to listen to some records while we eat?"

"Sure, that'd be nice. Play the two records I brought you and anything else you'd like."

Olivia put on Glenn's two records and a few more of her own, and they munched on the delicious popcorn and drank the steaming hot chocolate, talking as they did so with the soft music in the background.

"Do you think Jessica's attitude is any better?" Glenn asked, as he raised his cup to his lips.

"Not a whole lot, I'm afraid." Olivia set down her cup and looked earnestly at Glenn. "You have to understand that every time she sees us together it's a reminder of David's betrayal."

"Yeah, I guess it is, but I didn't mean for it to be like this. I didn't know he was married."

"Well, I believe she's thinking of joining the Y.W.C.A. They are beginning some new programs for young women, and they have a great cafeteria. One of Jessica's friends invited her to join, so maybe it will help take her mind away from it," she said hopefully.

"I hope it does, for her sake and ours," he replied, looking soberly at her. They had finished their refreshments and Olivia left the tray to return to the kitchen later. The record player had stopped playing, and both were silent, lost in their own thoughts for a few minutes.

Glenn shot back his cuff to look at his watch. "I guess I'd better shove off before long," he told her, knowing that the hour was getting late for the girls who had to get up early for work. He pulled her close and kissed her, putting his hand into her blouse to touch her intimately as he had before. Somehow his caresses seemed to soothe all her fears and calm any lingering doubts as long as he was with her. But when he was no longer there, the fears came stealing back into her mind, causing her to feel uncertain and insecure again—unsure of herself and her instincts, and afraid to trust her own judgment. She had always bowed to Jessica's advice—never knowing anything else—until her self-confidence had failed to take root and grow. Consequently, her emotions had not matured in the normal way. Without realizing it, Jessica had over-protected Olivia and kept her too long a child, not allowing Olivia to stand alone to make her own decisions.

Glenn kissed her several more times, and Olivia wished that things could always be like this between them, only without complications. Finally Glenn moved his arm from around her, and reached for his coat that lay beside him.

"I'd better go," he said, sliding his arms into his coat sleeves. "Thanks for the popcorn and hot chocolate. I enjoyed it very much."

"It wasn't much," Olivia shrugged, standing up as Glenn did. He gave her another kiss at the front door.

"I'll give you a call in a day or so. Maybe we can go to a movie or something." He smiled at her before he closed the screen door.

"Good night," Olivia said through the screen door. He threw up his hand at her, and she returned the wave before closing and locking the front door.

Olivia carried the tray back to the kitchen, passing Jessica seated on her bed filing her nails.

"You know he doesn't care anything about you, don't you?" she spoke bitterly to Olivia. Olivia stopped, not knowing what to say. Jessica's statement tore into her already shaky confidence, destroying her newly sprouted trust and causing her stomach to churn with fear and uncertainty. She carried the tray on into the kitchen and set it on the counter, wishing she could put her hands over her ears to keep Jessica's statement from echoing in her mind. *Was Jessica right? Did Glenn really care nothing for her?* Suddenly she was very tired, wanting nothing but to escape into the oblivion of sleep to still the taunting voice that kept ringing in her ears. Leaving the dishes for morning, she got ready for bed numbly, feeling like a puppet that is being pulled this way and that, without any power of its own.

The next few days passed uneventfully, with Olivia and Jessica following their accustomed routines of work, eating, and sleeping. They still were not saying much to each other, but at least they were speaking. After the third day had passed with no call from Glenn, Olivia began to feel anxious. Tension kept her on edge and her nerves were ready to snap. Glenn had promised to call her but the phone remained stubbornly silent. Olivia hadn't revealed to Jessica that Glenn had said he'd telephone but the suspense was wearing. She was afraid that her state of mind would give her away, but refused to let her frustration show.

The following morning Jessica finally spoke up. "What's happened to Glenn? He hasn't been around lately." She looked at Olivia over the breakfast table, her eyebrows raised in sarcasm.

"H-He's been busy this week. He said a lot would be going on but he might get a chance to come over for a while," she fabricated quickly.

"Oh?" Jessica asked, her expression one of disbelief.

"Yes, but he—he'll probably call me tonight," returned Jessica, attempting to inject a note of confidence into her voice that she didn't feel. Jessica didn't answer, letting her knowing expression silently express the taunting doubt in her mind.

Olivia turned away from the table. She picked up her dishes to stack them in the sink, ran hot water over them, and added dish detergent, watching the soap bubbles foaming over her plate, cup, and saucer. Jessica brought the remaining dishes from the table along with the silverware.

"If you ask me, I think he's just stringing you along before dropping you," Jessica threw over her shoulder as she started into the bedroom. Olivia leaned over the sink, her eyes closed to hold back the tears that threatened to fall. *Was Jessica speaking the truth?* Feeling the old familiar doubt and uncertainty seeping into her mind and emotions, she raised her head and opened her eyes, still battling her tears as she washed and rinsed the dishes before stacking them into the drainer to dry. She wouldn't let Jessica see her like this! She stilled her expression to one of calm indifference before entering the bedroom. Jessica had almost finished dressing.

"When he calls you again—and that's an if—you ought to break it off before he does," Jessica advised, slipping her feet into her shoes, holding on to the closet doorknob as she did so. Olivia refused to show any emotion, and began removing her housecoat. She'd already made her bed, so she dropped the housecoat onto it before going into the bathroom.

"I'll decide what to do when he calls me," she replied, as she shut the door behind her.

If Glenn were indeed stringing her along, as Jessica had predicted, she'd die if he broke up with her first. As much as it would hurt, she'd prefer being the one to call a halt rather than it being the other way around. This not knowing where she stood with Glenn, and Jessica's constant barbs were tying her up in knots. Anything was better than this uncertainty and confusion. *Had Glenn lost interest in her? Was he attempting to end their relationship?* She stepped into the shower. The stinging hot water made her feel more relaxed, and she stood under the spray for a few extra minutes, feeling a little of the tension drain away before stepping out to dry off.

He'd better call tonight with a good reason for breaking his word. This is the second time he's done that. She began dressing for work. She made it through the day, but that nagging uncertainty and indecision still lingered. *What should she do if he did call? Could she really trust him after his standing her up twice?*

That evening she entered the apartment feeling a sick tightness in her chest and with her stomach churning with dread. She wanted the phone to ring, but she equally feared it. She and Jessica had a quick meal of sausage, grits, toast, and applesauce. It was an appropriate meal, for the afternoon had been decidedly colder as Olivia walked from the bus stop the few blocks home to the apartment. After making short work of the dishes, Olivia started into the bedroom when the telephone jangled abruptly. Swallowing hard, she walked over to pick it up with trembling fingers.

"Hello," she answered trying to keep her voice cool and steady.

"Hi, Olivia. How are you tonight? I guess you wonder why I haven't called. I had a few things to take care of. You know how it is. Things can pile up on your sometimes, but I apologize for not calling you. I know I should have, and I'm sorry I didn't before now. Is it okay if I come by for a little while? I'd like to see you," she heard Glenn's familiar voice speaking through the receiver.

"Fine," she replied, and they each hung up.

Olivia suddenly felt a strange hardness come over her. Glenn's excuses sounded flimsy, and she made up her mind at once what she was going to do as soon as he came. Not stopping to think it over, she impulsively went into the living room. She was glad Jessica was still in the bathroom. Hearing the shower, she opened the drawer of the chest that held the phonograph records and pulled out the two on top. Next, she got out the photograph album and removed several snapshots. She was ready and waiting when Glenn rang the doorbell. Opening the door to him, she stood by as he walked into the living room.

"Hi. Did you miss me?" Glenn asked, as he dropped a quick kiss on her lips. Shutting the door behind him, she joined him on the sofa.

"Hello, Glenn," she replied calmly. She smelled the cold air and his brand of after-have lotion as she sat down by him. He looked at her with his special expression, searching her face as if trying to read her thoughts. She faltered for a moment, but then hardened her heart.

"Glenn, I think it's best if we don't see each other any more," she told him, handing him his records, and the pictures David had taken of the both of them together on several different occasions. He looked down at them and then into her face, his expression sobering, and studied her silently for a few moments.

"So it's all over but the shouting," he stated, still looking at her with regret. She nodded her head and looked away, not wishing to see his expression any more. He sat looking at the records and snapshots for a moment longer, and then picked them up. He stood and stared at her with that expression of solemn regret. She stood, also, and watched him turn away to leave. Neither of them spoke. He opened the door and walked out. Closing the door behind him she refused to think further, stoically closing her mind against any thoughts of him, and went into the bedroom.

Jessica had on her gown and robe and was toweling her hair dry.

"Did you break up with him?" she asked Olivia, her expression one of intense satisfaction.

"Yes. I gave him his records and pictures." For a moment, she wondered at Jessica's keen interest, and she felt a brief regret and sorrow, torn with a moment of questioning. *Did she do the right thing?* Then she stiffened her resolve and wouldn't let herself think about it any longer.

Jessica joined the Y.W.C.A. along with Olivia. Classes on good grooming, hygienic skin and hair care, healthful eating and exercise, and proper etiquette were offered both mornings and evenings. Dances were held on Saturday nights. Some of the airmen from the nearby Air Force Base attended with some of the junior Hostesses from the USO Club. For the working young women a special program along with lunch was offered each month. The girls could get their lunch from the lunchroom, bring it with them into the assembly room, and enjoy a break from their regular routine. A boarding house was conveniently available for girls who lived nearby and worked in the city and went home on the weekends.

The lunchroom fare was superb. Their chicken pie was one of Olivia's favorites. It had become a popular and well-attended group, and Jessica and Olivia enjoyed it. Olivia also enjoyed the Saturday evening entertainment and had become an expert dancer when she drew a good partner for the slow dances.

Then came a day that Olivia would long remember. It was another of the lunch hour meetings, and all seemed to be going as usual—lunch followed by the program for the day. Olivia's attention was focused on the speaker. She admired the woman's attractive outfit and self-confident poise. Suddenly, the young woman leading the program looked over to a table several rows away from Olivia, smiled widely, and announced, "We have an exciting bit of news to share with our group today. One of our members has recently received a diamond, and is engaged to PFC Glenn Havird from the nearby Air Force Base. Allyne, would you stand, please?"

Olivia sat as if frozen, and her heart thudded in such hard beats it seemed to suffocate her. She felt as if she were the object of attention rather than Allyne, who was happily going from one girl to another to show off her diamond. Waves of shock, humiliation, and shamed pride rolled over Olivia, and she felt as if every eye was on her in pity and scorn. Although it was she who had broken up with Glenn only three months ago, she felt they were considering the shoe to be on the other foot—that Glenn had discarded her for someone else. It seemed unreal that he could be marrying Allyne Simmons! Why, she was years older—even if she was still a Junior Hostess at the USO Club! Olivia wished she could disappear, find somewhere to hide, but she couldn't. She had to force herself to smile and pretend nothing was wrong. She felt dazed and betrayed, as if part of her had died, and been destroyed forever.

Then the thought came to her. *This must be the way that Jessica felt when she learned that David Winters was married. She couldn't have him because he belonged to someone else. I couldn't have Glenn because I turned him away, afraid to trust him, to take the risk of becoming vulnerable to another person. I listened to Jessica instead of to my heart. I was too frightened to emerge from my cocoon to become a butterfly—destined to remain unborn and imprisoned rather than daring to spread my wings to the sunlight and freedom. I failed him and he turned to someone who had the courage to trust him. I lost him because I was afraid to love him.*

NOW AND FOREVER

Ella met him on a blind date. Mutual friends arranged their first meeting, and they agreed that a double date would be best. They decided to go to a drive-in movie to see *The Ten Commandments,* with Charlton Heston as Moses.

Ella wore her favorite dress, a pastel green cotton and polyester with lace trim. Burt and Margaret sat in the front seat and Ella and James sat in the back. At the intermission, she and Margaret went to the ladies room to freshen up from the warm evening. Ella checked her appearance in the mirror. Her hair had behaved itself for once, after having been freshly washed and set, and she felt pleased at her reflection.

Margaret looked nice too. She and Margaret served as Junior Hostesses together at the USO Club.

"Have you been to the USO Club lately, Margaret?"

"No. I don't go too much these days. Have you?"

"No. I guess I got tired of it. It was always the same old thing—not enough men and too many girls."

"I know what you mean," Margaret said with a grin.

Margaret was a little slow, and sometimes it was hard to keep a conversation going with her. Ella felt sorry for her and tried to befriend her. She would always sit with her rather than sitting alone when things got dull at the NCO club dances.

"I guess we'd better get back. Burt and James will think we got lost," Ella said. Since each had freshened her lipstick and powdered her nose there was no reason to delay any longer.

"Yes, I guess so. We wouldn't want them to come looking for us."

Margaret had used her occasional sense of humor, and Ella laughed as they began their walk back to the car. The intermission was just ending. She tried not to look too closely at the cars they passed on their way.

Drive-in movies had earned the name of "passion pits" and Ella was afraid of what she might see. The area around the concession stand and the restrooms had adequate light but, with the exception of the scattered outdoor lights, the rest of the parking lot was dark.

They both stumbled a little as they reached their car, and Burt and James opened their doors so the girls could slide into their seats.

Ella felt comfortable with James. She had felt embarrassed before with other young men who had tried to come on too strong, but James was easy to talk with and kept his distance, for which she was grateful. Since the movie had started again, they didn't attempt any more conversation but kept their attention on the screen.

After the movie had ended and as they pulled out of the lot to head for home, Ella glanced at her watch. It was one o'clock in the morning! She'd never stayed out this late before, even though she was twenty-four years old. Margaret was older than she, but Ella wasn't sure of her age.

"It was a good movie, wasn't it?" she asked the others.

"Yes, but I don't see how they made some of the scenes. I liked the one where the Red Sea parted to allow the Israelites to walk across on dry land. It appeared that the Egyptians were going to catch up with them until the last minute." Burt answered her, glancing at her in his rear view mirror.

He was a country boy from the state of Texas, so he, too, was easy to talk with. His was a plain, uncomplicated nature, but he liked to poke fun at James and Margaret. He'd tried joking with Ella, too, and she was surprised how easy it was to answer him in kind. On the way home, they made arrangements to go to the mountains the next day. They decided to visit Toxaway Falls, located in upper South Carolina next to the North Carolina line. The falls were not extremely high, as were some of the waterfalls in the area, but they were clear and wide and the water fell over a solid bed of rock into the river below.

"You can slide down the falls," Burt informed the group, "but the rocks are hard on where you sit down." They all laughed at him.

"Bring your bathing suits so we can go into the water," James chimed in.

Ella had a new black, one-piece bathing suit that she was looking forward to wearing. It was really the only one she owned, since she didn't have much occasion to wear one. She was glad now that she'd decided to purchase it. Her thoughts went back to her and James' conversation last night. They had talked about each other's background as they drove to and from the drive-in theatre, and she was interested in learning more about him. She thought back to the late drive home.

"Doris will wonder where I am. I've never been this late before. She's four years older than me, and still looks after me like I'm a child. She pretty much raised me for much of my life so I guess she will always feel responsible for me."

"Are your parents both dead?"

"No, my mother's still living. She's in a nursing home because she has arthritis and isn't able to walk. She has to be in a wheel chair when she's not in bed. My father died when I was ten years old. Are both your parents living?"

"Yes. We live in the country. My father raises hogs and has a few cows and chickens. He built his own chicken house for them. Some of the people around us have two or three large chicken houses, but he could only afford to build one. There are two poultry processing plants near us so it takes a lot of houses to grow enough chickens to keep the processing plants in business," he explained.

"Do you have any sisters or brothers?"

"Yes. I have one sister, four-and-a half years older, who's married, with two little "curtain climbers." Rusty is eight and Al is almost four. When I go home from the base for the weekend they both want me to play with them. I usually baby sit for my sister and her husband to go out. The kids and I usually end up having wrestling matches and pillow fights."

"So you boys play rough, huh?"

"I have to get rough sometimes to get them to calm down. They can get pretty wild."

They pretty much had the same background, so it made it easy for them to understand each other. She'd lived in the country until her father died and could relate to many of the stories James told.

"My father grew vegetables for his farm business during the day and worked in a cotton mill at night. My twin sister and I helped him with the vegetables. His biggest crop was okra. We had to wear long-sleeved shirts, gloves, and straw hats to protect us from the both the sun and the okra. If you don't protect your arms and hands, they will sting something awful from handling the okra pods and brushing against the leaves."

"My mother always has a big garden, and freezes or cans most of the vegetables. She makes cucumber and peach pickles. Some of the peach orchard owners will let people come into their orchards to pick the leftover peaches when they have finished picking their crop. We have our own apple trees, and she cans or freezes them, too. Then she makes all kinds of jellies and jams. She's really busy during the summer."

"It sounds like it. But then you have plenty to eat for the winter," Ella said.

She decided to change the subject to a more personal one.

"You and Burt are in the Air Force together, aren't you? What kind of work do you do?"

"I'm an aircraft engine mechanic, working on aircraft engines on the C-124 cargo plane called the Globemaster."

"Do you do a lot of flying?"

"Yeah, quite a bit, I guess. It's mostly TDY trips. That stands for temporary duty trips. I work with a flight crew of men and we've been together to fix downed airplanes, if we can, or if not, completely replace the engine, or engines. We've been to Germany, Italy, Cypress, South America, and Lebanon, just to name a few places."

"You like flying, don't you?"

"Yes. I wanted to be a pilot but I couldn't because I'm color blind."

"Oh, that's too bad. It's mostly men who are color blind, isn't it?"

"Yeah. I have to compensate for it and make an extra effort that other people don't. For instance, all the wiring to the engines is color-coded. I have to be extra careful to be sure I know which wire is which. A person who isn't color blind doesn't have the same trouble."

"Well, it seems to me that you're a pretty successful person to be able to compensate for a handicap and still do a good job. I'm sure it isn't easy, but you've managed to overcome it. I think that's very commendable."

"Thanks!"

By this time they had arrived at the duplex apartment Ella shared with her older sister. Burt shut off the engine, and Ella waited for James to come around to open her door.

"At least he has good manners," she thought.

Burt and Margaret were still in the front seat. They were going to drop Margaret off on the way back to the base, as she lived in the area.

"It was nice meeting you, Burt. I had a nice time. Margaret, I'll see you tomorrow." Ella waved to them as she began to walk up the walkway to her apartment.

Burt and Margaret returned the wave, and James shut her door and joined her side to walk her to the door.

"I had a nice time, James, and I enjoyed meeting you. I'll look forward to tomorrow. I'll probably wear my bathing suit under my shorts and shirt because I'm not sure if they have a bathhouse there."

"I've never been there before so I'm afraid I can't answer that. I'll see you tomorrow though. It was nice meeting you too. So until tomorrow, good night."

"Good night."

As Ella had expected, Doris was surprised and a little worried that she was so late returning home.

"It's after one o'clock in the morning, Ella. I was worried. I thought you had car trouble or something."

"No, it was nothing like that. We went to see *The Ten Commandments,* which is a three-hour movie not including an intermission. It was a good movie, but I'm sorry it was so long. I didn't mean to worry you. We decided to go to Toxaway Falls tomorrow and go swimming. I thought I'd wear my bathing suit under my shirt and shorts since I don't know if there's any place to change. Do you think that would be okay?"

"Yes, I think so. If they don't have a bathhouse you can hardly go into the woods to change."

"That's what I thought. Well, I guess we'd better get some sleep. Church comes early tomorrow and my Sunday school class will be expecting me. They're short of help and those kids can get rowdy. I took the class because they needed another teacher. Those preschoolers are a handful. I've had problems knowing how to deal with the children, and they sense that and take advantage of my inexperience. There are two other teachers but sometimes one of them has to miss.

They'd begged me so hard to take the class I hated to say no. It's hard to keep the children's attention for very long, and when the department leader teaches the lesson, my inexperience prevents me from knowing how to be firm but pleasant to keep them quiet. I would enjoy the class if I knew more about working with children."

"Well, experience is the best teacher, they say. You'll probably learn more as you go along."

"I hope so. Well, good night, Doris. And again, I'm sorry about making you worry."

"It's okay. Good night."

Ella was ready when Burt and the others came by to pick her up for their planned trip to the mountains. She climbed into the car and greeted everyone.

"Are you planning on going into the water?" Ella asked Margaret.

"I'll probably just wade out a little way. I don't know how to swim."

"I don't either, but I wore my bathing suit under my clothes just in case. If I know boys, they'll probably splash us and we'll get wet. And they probably know how to swim."

Ella turned to James. "Can you swim?"

"Yeah. When I was a little boy we'd go to the creek and go out in the boat. The creek was deep enough back then so you could go swimming. My daddy threw me into the water and I had to swim or go under. That's how I learned to swim. The creek has gone down now, though, because so many people around us have built ponds for their cows."

"I've always heard that's the wrong way to teach children to swim."

"Well, I've played in the creek my whole life and I already knew how to float."

"Oh, well, I guess it worked for you then, didn't it?"

They were nearing the mountains and Toxaway Falls wasn't too far ahead.

The air was cooler from the abundance of trees on each side of the road as they drew nearer to the mountains. Burt turned off onto the road that led to Toxaway Falls. Soon he pulled into a clearing where they could both see and hear the loud splashing from the water as it fell over the rocks to the river below.

The men stripped to their bathing suits and dashed for the water. While their attention was on the falls, Ella hurriedly pulled off her shirt and shorts. Margaret rolled her pedal pushers to above her knees. They ventured carefully on tender, bare feet to the edge of the water. There were abundant tiny rocks to torture their sensitive feet so they had to proceed with caution.

By the time they arrived, the men had already slid down the falls a couple of times and shouted encouragingly to the girls, "Come on, the water's great!"

Margaret and Ella stepped into the water and shivered at its icy temperature. They walked out farther, despite the chill, and found their bodies warming up a bit as they reached the open sunshine, leaving the shade of the woods that surrounded the river and the falls. Soon they grew accustomed to it and splashed around a bit as they watched the men and other hardy souls who were sliding down the falls.

Ella didn't want to get her hair wet and neither did Margaret. After a while spent walking in the frothy water of the falls, they grew tired and decided to head back to the river's edge, away from the pebbled area to the bank where the leaves and pine straw from the trees made a softer surface for their bare feet.

Burt came out of the water and headed for his car. He returned with a large watermelon. Carrying it over to where the girls stood, he set it on a tree stump and James soon joined them. The men were pondering how they would cut it, as neither had brought a suitable knife.

"I've got a pocket knife," James offered. He walked over to where he'd laid his pants and pulled out his pocketknife.

"My daddy always says if he's got his pants on he's got his pocketknife.

I guess I'm like him to that extent." They all laughed.

Handing it to Burt to figure out how to cut the watermelon, he rejoined the girls where they stood a few feet away. Ella began to feel uncomfortable because he kept looking at the top part of her bathing suit, which was modestly enough cut, and then she got irritated.

You'd think he'd never seen a girl in a bathing suit before.

Margaret had tied the ends of her blouse together and it made a nice enough outfit with the rolled up pedal pushers.

Burt finally managed to haggle out pieces of the melon for each of them, and they held it in their hands to eat. Ella thought how like boys they were not to think of bringing a bigger knife with which to cut the watermelon.

"You ready to go back into the water, James?" Burt asked, wiping his mouth with the back of his hand. He'd have plenty of water to wash off the sticky juice when he was under the falls.

"In a minute. I want to dispose of these watermelon rinds."

James stacked them on top of each other, walked a short distance into the woods, and threw each piece as far as he could. Then he came back to the others.

"Burt's worn a hole in the back of his swimming trunks from sliding down the falls," he confided to the girls, laughing at his friend's antics as he once more slid down the falls.

"Pretty soon he's going to have the whole seat of his trunks worn out," he said, laughing again. They all watched in amusement as Burt continued to slide down the falls. He was enjoying himself as only a country boy could.

At last Burt grew tired and was ready to leave. With the exception of Margaret, who was already dressed, they all put on their clothing and started home. Ella and James once more sat in the back seat and James confided to Ella, "Burt was wondering if you knew another girl he could ask out. He doesn't want to go out with Margaret again."

As they started around the winding road down the mountain, Ella thought of her friend Janice. She and Janice usually ate lunch together once a week, sometimes at the Clock Drive-In Restaurant, or at Morrison's Cafeteria, which they especially enjoyed.

"I have a friend I meet for lunch every week. I'll ask her if she'd like to go out with him. She lives at the YWCA during the week and goes home on the weekend. She lives near Greer, on the outskirts of Greenville."

"Yes, I know Greer," James replied. "Thanks. I appreciate it, and I'm sure he will too. He just got back to Donaldson after being stationed in Germany. He's in my barracks at the base, and I kept his car for him while he was away so the battery wouldn't go dead. I hope to get a car, myself, before long.

I want a black '51 Ford. There's one for sale at a car lot near the base that looks pretty good. I'll probably have to fix it up some, but since I'm a car mechanic, too, that won't be a problem."

"How did you learn car mechanics?"

"My daddy taught me. We Millers just seem to have a natural mechanical knack. He taught me everything I know. I've helped him put a new motor in his car, put in new brakes, brake linings, turned the drums, and fixed carburetors, just to name a few things."

"That's wonderful! It sure saves you a lot of money, doesn't it?"

"Sure does. All I have to do is buy new parts, if I can't fix the old ones, and put them in. It saves a bundle on labor. That usually costs as much or more than the parts do to fix it with."

Ella was enjoying talking with James as they traveled down the picturesque mountain road toward Greenville, her hometown. Donaldson Air Force base was located on the lower outskirts of town. It was built during the Second World War as a training base.

She and James seemed to be able to carry on a conversation on any subject that came up between them. She was a good listener as he explained things about his work at the base on C-124 Globemasters. He was crazy about airplanes, and enjoyed his job as an aircraft engine mechanic. It was evident that he was dedicated to doing his best work because he realized that other men's lives depended on his skill and training. She could also see his dedication to the Air Force, as well as to his job, and although she hadn't known him long, she had a deep respect for his evident character and sense of responsibility.

He had also told her about growing up on his father's farm.

"When I was fifteen years old, my parents had a chance to go to the Air Force base in Abilene, Texas, where my uncle was stationed. He and his wife had come home to visit, and wanted to take my parents back with them, go on to Mexico to see the Alamo and cross the Rio Grande. I told them to go because they would never get a chance like that again; I had my whole life ahead of me and would have a chance to go to a lot of places.

We had big chickens then, almost big enough for fryers, and I had to stay home to take care of them.

They went, and had a good time. They were gone a week, and I stayed home by myself. I wasn't afraid, though, because I had plenty to do with making sure the chickens had plenty of food and water, and caring for the hogs and mules. I had to shuck a bushel basket of corn every evening for the hogs, and if a storm came up, I had to go into the chicken house to try to keep them from suffocating each other. You see, thunder and lightning frightens them, and they'll all pile into a corner on top of each other. If I didn't dig down to keep them separated, those on the bottom would suffocate to death. They represented a lot of money."

Ella was rapidly learning how much she and James had in common. She, too, had lived in the country until she was ten years old. Her father had grown vegetables and sold them to a small grocery store whose owner he'd known for many years. He'd grown tomatoes, green beans, butterbeans, corn, turnip greens and turnips, and okra, his biggest seller.

She felt that since they'd grown up in similar surroundings, it helped her to feel comfortable with him. As always, she found the trip home seemed shorter than had the ride to their destination.

"Have you ever noticed that a trip home always seems shorter than the one to where you've been? I've always felt so, anyway."

"Yeah. You're anxious to get to where you're going, but coming home it's all behind you so you seem to arrive home sooner."

"That must be it. Oh, and I'll talk to Janice and see if she's interested in going out with Burt and let you know."

"Okay. I'll call you Thursday evening. Don't you and she usually have lunch together every Wednesday?" James asked.

"Yes. It's become a bit of a tradition. I'll let you know what she decides."

They pulled up in front of her house, which was closest on their way home, and James climbed out to escort her to her front door. Ella had already said her farewells so she simply waved to Margaret as she looked back.

"Ella may have another girl friend for you to go out with; a friend who lives at the YWCA and goes to her home in Greer on the weekends," James told Burt in a low voice through the open car window when he returned. Margaret was a little hard of hearing, but he didn't want to take the chance that she would overhear their conversation.

"Oh, that's swell. Maybe we can double date again. Margaret's a nice girl, but she's a little old and settled for me," Burt said.

"Ella told me that she lives at home with her parents. Since none of their other relatives are living, they only have each other. It's kind of sad."

Janice did begin going out with Burt, and Ella and James continued to date each other. He kissed her at the end of their third date when he brought her home. It seemed like the perfect ending to a wonderful evening.

"May I see you tomorrow night, Ella?" he asked as he held her hand.

"Well, I really need to do some things around the house. I have some clothes that need washing, and I want to shampoo my hair."

"Oh, all right. How about the next night?"

"As far as I know it's open. You can call me if you like."

"Okay. I'll call you early and maybe we can go out to eat at Capri's."

"That sounds nice. I'll talk to you then, and we'll see."

"Well, good night, Ella."

"Good night, James."

James did call her as promised, and they decided to eat at Capri's and go to a movie afterwards at the base theatre.

Ella was not a big eater, and couldn't eat all her spaghetti. It was a huge plate. James must have been hungry from working hard on the flight line. He finished his with no trouble.

"I'm sorry," she said, "I'm just not a big eater, I guess."

"I can see that. It must be why you're so slim. You'll notice I didn't say skinny. There is a difference. A slight one, but a difference nonetheless." He smiled at her fondly. "I don't mind. At the chow hall, or the mess hall as we call it, you learn to eat fast. They only give you thirty minutes to go there, eat, and get back to work on time. I guess I've just gotten into the habit of eating fast."

The movie was a new one. The service men were lucky because the base theatre got all the new releases before the theatres in town. The admission price was only twenty-five cents. Ella was amazed at the low cost and enjoyed the movie, despite the fact that James held her hand and toyed with her ring during the movie. He turned it around on her finger and caressed her hand, which distracted her. She tried to ignore it, but she found it hard to ignore the feeling of sexual attraction she felt toward him. Pretending to behave as though her full attention was on the movie screen, she enjoyed the feel of his hand on hers, the way he stroked her fingers one at a time, and continued to turn the ring around her finger.

After the movie, they rode to his favorite hangout near the base. It was a service station, and James was well acquainted with the owner/station manager because he bought all his gas there. He introduced Ella to Mr. McMeekin, or Mac as most of his friends and customers knew him. James filled up his tank with gas and then headed to a bar and grill restaurant a short distance away. He went inside and came out with a cola for each of them.

"They sell beer," he told her, "and get a lot of business from the servicemen at Donaldson. Sometimes they get into fights and the MP's, or Military Police, have to come out and settle it."

He headed toward the outskirts of the base perimeter to a wooded area and drove down a deserted road. He parked the car and Ella looked at him uncertainly, not sure what was going to happen.

He pulled her close to him and began to kiss her. She liked the feel of his lips on hers. They felt soft at first and then, as he grew more passionate, he began to deepen his kisses and his lips became firmer and more persuasive. He slipped his hand under her dress and rubbed his hand up and down her leg, reaching up to her inner thigh. Eventually he reached the edge of her panties. She squeezed her legs tightly, refusing to let his hand become more intimate. He took her hand and pressed it against the hardness of his arousal, holding it tightly against him so that she could feel the pulsation through his pants.

"You're not a tease, are you?" he asked, his mouth seeking hers again.

He took her hand again and rubbed it against his erection, taking deep, fast breaths. She pulled away, not wanting to touch him so intimately and unsure just what to do. She'd never been in a situation like this before, even though she was three and a half years older than he. She'd led a very sheltered life with just Doris there most of the time. But Doris had an ingrained sense of responsibility toward Ella and her sister, and she knew it would be difficult for her to let go when the time came. She advised her to wait until she had a ring on her finger before indulging in kissing and "petting" as it was known then. Ella was totally inexperienced in matters of this kind. But her faith in James was so pure, without doubt or wavering, that she was willing to explore further into their relationship.

As he'd previously told her, he'd spent the night with a prostitute in Germany where he'd been stationed for six months. He said it had only been one time, but she felt a little jealous and cheated. He assured her it hadn't meant anything. She instinctively knew that it had been his first time.

When he saw she wouldn't agree, he got out of the car, his face drawn in pain, and relieved himself. She was learning and seeing things that were utterly foreign to her. She felt both revulsion and a feminine compassion for him. When he got back in the car he turned to her.

"I'm sorry. I shouldn't have done that. Some girls get a fellow all excited and then leave him hanging. It's very painful. They're what men call a tease."

"Oh."

"You've never been with a man like that before, have you?"

"No, I haven't."

"I love you, Ella. I don't want to mess this up. What I'm trying to say is, will you marry me?"

"But it's too soon," she protested. "We've only known each other three weeks,"

"It doesn't take long to know when you meet the right girl, and you're the right girl for me. I don't want someone who's been from man to man. I've met a lot of girls around the base like that, most of who were married. When their husbands had to go overseas on TDY, they went out with other men. I've even had them come on to me. I've seen a lot and talked to the other guys. Some of them can't trust their wives. I have a buddy who is sure that his youngest son isn't his."

"How awful!"

"I'll bet you've never seen a man without his clothes on, have you?"

"No, of course not!"

"I've heard the guys say that some girls are frightened on their wedding night. They're afraid when they see their husband naked, and when he approaches he looks so big that they don't know how he can get inside them. I don't want you to be frightened on our wedding night."

He unzipped his pants and showed her his maleness. She felt a mixture of numb surprise, a strange sense of resignation, and of acceptance. Now she knew what a man looked like and she felt she would never feel afraid around men again; she now knew all there was to know about a man. *So this is what women have to put up with.*

She watched with a strange sense of unreality as James got down on his knees before her, and pulled up her skirt. She who had been taught that nice girls didn't do such things was doing them.

"Pull down your panties," he instructed her.

Still feeling that all this wasn't real, she obeyed and pulled up her slip and skirt still farther so that she could get to her panties, and slipped them down. He eased himself into her a little at a time and began to move inside her. Suddenly he pulled himself out before ejaculation, and reached into his back pocket for his handkerchief. He cleaned himself with it.

So that's how it's done. It didn't last long enough for me to feel anything, and, anyway, I don't even know what it's supposed to feel like. Perhaps next time will be better...but what am I saying?"

"You'll probably bleed a little bit tomorrow."

She felt dazed, still not believing any of this was real. She was totally out of her element even though she would soon be twenty-five. He was more emotionally and mentally mature then she was although she was three-and-a-half years older. She supposed that was why she hadn't questioned him, but went where he led in their relationship because their personalities blended together so well that she felt comfortable with him. She'd made a conscious choice and felt no regrets or self-recriminations. The bond that held them together was now tighter than ever.

"You're okay, aren't you? I didn't hurt you, did I?"

"No, I don't think so. It just felt strange and new, sort of tight. It hurt just a little bit for a minute." She didn't realize that he hadn't entered her all the way so that she would possibly have felt some sensation of pleasure. It still was difficult for her to fathom that she was here in a car on "lover's lane" with a man. She'd been taught that nice girls did not park, kiss and "pet," and here she was doing that very thing. Her trust in him still did not waver. They belonged together, of that she was certain. That's all she needed to know.

"You may be a little sore. But I'll take care of you. If you get pregnant I'll marry you."

Strangely, she'd never even thought of the possibility of getting pregnant or if they'd have to get married.

"You're not going to break up with me, are you?" he asked.

"No. I just think we need to start over and really get to know each other."

He looked at her with uncertainty, as if he feared that she was really going to break up with him. Maybe he'd rushed things too fast.

Both were silent during the ride to her apartment. He came around to open her car door, and she stepped out. Holding her hand as they walked to the steps and ascended to the porch, he pulled her close, looking at her as if he was still afraid that she would say goodbye forever.

A new sense of protection and affection entered her heart, and she put her hands on his chest to comfort him.

"I'm going home this weekend," he said. "Mama's not doing well and I promised her I'd help her rake and take the leaves out of her yard. We'll probably have several trailer loads to haul off with the tractor."

They say that if a man is good to his mother, he'll be good to his wife.

"Will you go to church Sunday?"

He'd already confided to her that he'd joined the church and was baptized when he was about ten years old.

"Yeah, I guess so. My sister and her husband and their two curtain climbers will probably be there to eat with us. Mama usually stays home so she can cook a big dinner for everyone."

"Well, good night. Have a nice weekend."

She turned to go, but he pulled her back to kiss her again. She felt his regret when he had to release her to go home. She went inside the duplex apartment she shared with her older sister.

I've got a lot of thinking to do. I need to pray about this, because I don't want to make a mistake.

She prayed that night in her bed that if she and James were meant to be together, the Lord would let her know. If he called her, she would take it as a sign that they were meant to be together. If he didn't call her, she would assume that it wasn't God's will for them to continue seeing one another or to get married.

Ella tried not to listen for the phone over the weekend, and kept looking to God to keep her calm and serene. She knew she had to trust Him to help her make the right decision. She went to church and to her preschool Sunday school class. As usual, they were full of energy, bursting at the seams when they were supposed to be sitting and paying attention. She still felt inadequate because she didn't know the children well enough to relate to them, and had not yet became familiar with the routine established by the department leader and the other class teacher. It was with a feeling of relief that she heard the bell signaling the end of the Sunday school hour.

That afternoon the phone rang. Ella had a premonition that it was James before she answered.

"Hey, what are you doing?"

She was happy to hear his deep voice

"Oh, not much of anything. How about you?"

"Well, we got Mama's yard cleaned up yesterday and I just got back to the base. Seemed like there was a mountain of leaves to rake. She has a lot of big oak trees, and they each have tons of leaves. I helped Daddy take them down to the hog pen and put them into the stables. That'll help keep them from getting in such a mess this winter. I just got through eating a big dinner. Mama made hot biscuits and we had coconut pie for dessert. She knows it's my favorite."

Maybe that's why you're a little overweight.

But she felt herself smile at the thought. He was so kind and had so many good qualities that they made up for it. She liked the deep dimple in his chin inherited from his father, and the dimples on each side of his mouth he'd also inherited from his dad.

His brown eyes and dark brown hair came from his father, also, and although not quite as tall as his father, he was more than a head taller than she. Not yet twenty-one, he was already getting a little bald, also like his father. She supposed his tendency to be a little heavy came from his mother's side of the family. He had his father's mouth, with lips a little full and shapely. But it wasn't just his looks that attracted her—it was the feeling of security he gave her, of steady dependability and steadfastness that she needed.

"Oh, that'll be nice. About the leaves in the hog stables, I mean. Does your father have many pigs?"

"Yeah, he has about thirty. Some are sows that he breeds every year. They're so fat he has to watch them closely when they have their piglets so they don't kill any when they lie down to nurse them. The sows sometime roll over on one or two and kill them accidentally. He also buys some pigs off the market and sells them for a profit as soon as they reach the right size."

"That's awful. The sows really lie down on some of their babies when they are nursing them? What on earth does he feed them to make them grow so big?"

"Mostly corn. He grows it, and then grinds the dry corn to mix with supplement feed. It has lots of the nutritional value that pigs need and it makes them fatten up sooner."

Ella was glad that he hadn't given up on her, and took it as a sign from God that they should continue their relationship.

"Want to go get a root beer float?" he asked.

"That sounds great."

"See you in about thirty minutes then?"

"Yes, that'll be fine."

James was prompt and she met him at the door. She'd always felt comfortable and at ease with him, and now it was even easier to share her thoughts with him. It was as though they belonged together, and she was now certain that they did.

They pulled up to the A & W drive-in restaurant. The carhop took their order and while they were waiting, an airplane flew overhead, coming in for a landing. It sounded as if it was right on top of them.

"We're not far from the base," James explained.

"You couldn't get a good look at it, but that was a C-124 Globemaster, the kind of plane I work on. Would you like to ride out to the base and see one when we finish our drinks?"

"Yes, I'd love to."

She was interested in his work and felt that they shared it together.

Their root beer floats arrived, and Ella thought the vanilla ice cream and root beer was a delicious combination.

"This is good."

She sipped hers through the straw until she got down to the bottom of the cup where the ice cream had settled. James handed her a plastic spoon from the tray outside his car window to finish up her ice cream.

"Thanks. This is the best part," Ella said, dipping into the root beer flavored ice cream with relish.

When they had finished eating, he drove her out to the Air Force base. She was surprised at how expansive it was.

"That's my barracks," he said, pointing to a two-story gray building as they passed it. Ella looked at it curiously.

"How many guys are in your barracks?"

"Well, it varies from eight to a dozen. Some guys are shipped out, and new ones come in. Usually it stays around ten or so."

He stopped at one of the hangars and they got out of the car.

"That's one of the planes I've been working on," he told her, directing her attention to a large airplane in front of the hangar.

"This is the flight line where we work. Sometimes we get to work inside if the weather is bad, but usually this is it."

The plane had four large engines and the nose was painted black. The inside of the plane looked immense. They walked up the huge ramp into the cargo area.

"What can it carry?"

"Oh, we've carried everything from jeeps to caterpillars and tanks. You'd be surprised how much it can hold."

"I'm not really surprised. It's so huge!"

"Yeah, it's pretty big. That's where we sit when we're flying."

He pointed to some bunk-like seats along the sides of the plane, closer to the front of the plane from the cargo area.

"Do you like to fly?"

"Yeah, I enjoy it. Sometimes if we're standing up and we hit an air pocket we'll be lifted off our feet, but we get used to it. I was in the top of my class in engine school. Anything to do with airplanes interests me."

Ella shared his interest and she was proud of his ability and chosen career field.

"I think it's wonderful that you are able to help to keep them flying. The C-124's are a special airplane to you, aren't they?"

"Yeah, they are. There's nothing like them. Ready to go?"

"If you are."

Truthfully, Ella was tired of walking on the concrete flight line. They'd seen several other different airplanes and she'd listened as he told her about them. His enthusiasm was contagious to Ella but, interesting as it was, she was getting tired.

"What time do you go to lunch?" he asked.

"Around twelve o'clock."

"May I pick you up for lunch tomorrow?"

"Yes, I'd like that."

"Okay. It's a deal. We'll have to go somewhere like The Clock drive-in for both of us to get back to work on time."

"Oh, that's fine. I can eat anything."

"I like barbecue sandwiches. They make good ones at the Clock." He smiled.

It was getting dark so James drove her home. Doris had left the front porch light on for her, and as they started up the steps to the front porch of the duplex apartment, moths and other bugs were beginning to surround the overhead light.

"Well, I'll see you tomorrow," he said with a wink.

"Okay."

He pulled her to him and kissed her. His lips were soft and tender and she liked the way they felt on hers. He wasn't rough or demanding, which was another of his characteristics that she liked.

He turned and walked down the steps to his car. She started inside, but paused to watch him back out of the driveway before she closed the door.

He had bought a '51 black Ford, which was his favorite model. If anything broke down, whether it was the engine, brakes, or anything else he could fix it. She was proud of his mechanical ability, and knew that he saved a lot of money and time by being able to make any repairs needed.

The next day at twelve o'clock she went out to the parking lot at work to find him waiting for her. She loved the fact that he was never late. In fact, he was usually early. She felt secure because he was always prompt—that he really wanted to be with her.

She climbed into the car after he'd opened the door for her, and they drove to The Clock drive-in restaurant. Everyone usually referred to it simply as The Clock.

As they drove through the lunch-hour traffic, he looked down at her. They had sat close to one another from their first date alone. When they weren't in heavy traffic he would often hold her hand in his, and she liked to lay her hand on his thigh. She could feel the muscles in his leg flex when he stepped on the brake. There was a closeness and intimacy between them that required no words. She felt their minds were so entwined each knew what the other was thinking, although she knew it was more than that—they were already so joined in heart and mind they were one. Her trust in him was complete, so much so that it never occurred to her to not to trust him. When she was much younger, twenty-one or so, she'd felt tense around a date if a silence fell between them; she'd felt that she had to say something to break it or he would feel bored and want to drop her. She'd had little self-confidence, and didn't know how to just relax and be herself so that they could get to know one another and enjoy being together.

Now she was enjoying her first experience of just being natural, relaxed, and close to someone without feeling she had to talk unless she had something to say.

"You know you haven't given me an answer yet. Are you going to marry me?"

"To tell you the truth, I feel like we're already married," she confessed, smiling at him through the sun's glare reflected on the car windows.

"Me, too. Let's pick out a ring tomorrow. I want everyone to know you belong to me."

"Okay. That'll be exciting. But you have to know that this is sort of a trial engagement, James. When you get back from Operation Deep Freeze, if we both feel the same way, I'll marry you."

The next day they met for lunch again, and went to the jeweler's to choose her ring. She looked at the many sizes and styles of diamonds, and chose the first one that had caught her eye. It was a diamond in a square setting, and as the light entered to reflect its facets, it flashed and looked larger than it really was, perfect in the white gold style. She knew she'd never find one that she'd like better. It was arranged that James would mail the money order to her for each month's payment, and as the jewelry store was close to her work she could go in to pay the jeweler each month.

After they had eaten their lunch, and while he was driving her back to work, she reflected on their relationship. Suddenly she Scripture verse she had heard many times regarding marriage came to her: "Therefore a man shall leave his father and his mother, and shall cleave unto his wife, and they shall be one flesh." She knew that God had established the institution of marriage and that it was intended to last until death.

James had explained to her that the sexual union made a man and woman married in the sight of God.

That must be the reason I feel we're already married and feel this deep commitment to him.

They went to his home one last time before he left for the South Pole. He brought his footlocker to the front porch and insisted that she paint his name and the address at which he would receive his mail at the Pole.

"You handwriting is better than mine," he said with a grin.

Soon after he left Donaldson Air Force Base to fly to the South Pole and the Operation Deep Freeze mission. He would be gone approximately three months.

She decided to take a Training Union class of six and seven-year-old children at her church on Sunday evenings to help the time go more quickly. This, coupled with her job, prevented her from dwelling on his absence.

She wrote to him almost every day. His letters to her, however, were sporadic due to the airmail delivery system. Some days she would receive two, three, or even four letters, and then it would be a week or so before she would get another.

In her letters to him she wrote about the children in her new class. She told him about a recent ploy she had discovered involving the children. They asked to be excused to use the bathroom, and then they would run up and down the hall screaming and causing a ruckus. Because of her inexperience, she had a hard time keeping them under control and ensuring that they stayed busy. She expressed her thoughts and frustrations to James, finding that whenever she put her thoughts onto the paper, she felt better about the situation and more inclined to make a change. Her letters to James were often full of her experiences with the children's antics and misbehavior.

The weeks flew by quickly, and suddenly one night the phone rang and his familiar voice echoed in her ear.

"Hi there, stranger! Can I come on over to see my favorite girl?"

"You're home early! Of course you can come over."

As soon as she opened the door for him to enter the apartment and felt his cold cheek on hers and the warmth of his kiss, all her doubts about marrying him were gone. She smiled at him as she grabbed his hand and led him into the apartment.

They sat on the sofa and he began to tell her of his experiences in the Antarctic wilderness. He told her about when he and his flight crew were stranded with their airplane for two or three days due to a whiteout, a fierce snowstorm that blew the snow so strongly that it was impossible to see anything. They had to crank the plane ever so often to keep the oil from freezing. He'd had some minor frostbite on his toes and fingers, but it had soon healed.

In his barracks at the Deep Freeze base, a kind of Quonset hut, he told her how the soldier on the bottom bunks would freeze, and the person on the top bunk would feel as if they were burning up due to the erratic temperatures in the hut. It always seemed as if he was either too hot or too cold, never anything in between.

He told her about the man who had been on the mission before he arrived. He was unloading a tractor from the belly of the plane and ran into a thin patch of ice. The man and the tractor fell into water that was so cold it would freeze a human being in a matter of seconds. It was useless to attempt to bring him up because of the danger of the thin ice and futility of trying to rescue the body. His back was still visible through the ice, an eerie sight he'd avoided whenever possible.

They began to talk about marriage, and he hugged her tightly when she agreed to marry him.

"I've got about a hundred dollars in my savings account," she offered.

That wouldn't seem like much in today's money, but in 1959 one hundred dollars went much farther. They both realized that they couldn't afford a big wedding, but it didn't matter. They were just excited to be together.

"I don't think you have to have blood tests in Georgia," James told her.

She didn't question his knowledge, so they decided to elope to Athens, Georgia, to get married. Her hundred dollars in savings was withdrawn and, after telling her two sisters of their plan, they packed a few things in a suitcase and left for their destination.

To their surprise, when they went to the Health Department for their marriage license, they learned that a blood test was a requirement in the state of Georgia. They had to wait twenty-four hours after taking their blood tests before they could receive their marriage license. They rented an inexpensive motel room, but because of his loud snoring and her state of excitement, she didn't sleep much that night.

After picking up the results of the blood tests from the Health Department, they went to the courthouse to apply for their marriage license. The Justice of the Peace, known as a Probate Judge in South Carolina, had authority to marry them, so they decided to get married in the courthouse.

The Justice of the Peace was an older gentleman and to her surprise and appreciation, he talked to them as if he were a licensed minister, giving them marriage counseling and advice prior to the service.

"Marriage is just what you make it," he told them.

She took his words to heart. She was determined to make it a lasting marriage, and realized the seriousness of the step she and James were taking. As the Justice of the Peace performed the marriage ceremony and she and James exchanged rings, she felt as happy as if they had been married in a church. It was a solemn occasion, and she knew she'd always remember it.

She vowed to do her best to help their marriage endure, and her feelings brought this silent promise to her heart—now and forever.

ABOUT THE AUTHOR

An interest in writing led the author to write about what she knew - her own life experiences. Writing them in third person, short story form, she'd not considered them memoirs until several years had passed. She'd written eight "stories."

An AuthorHouse services representative, Brian Mattox, approached her about a special promotion available. Lack of funds made her unable to reciprocate.

She talked to God, "Lord, if it's your will for me to publish my book, You'll have to make it possible." Days later, a company who'd employed her forty-three years earlier informed her that she had a small pension fund due her! Immediately she called Brian and set wheels rolling to get published.

www.ingramcontent.com/pod-product-compliance
Lightning Source LLC
Chambersburg PA
CBHW020421290526
45785CB00002B/662